CALIFORNIA MFT

Study Guide

2024-2025

- 📓 **Note-Taking Techniques:** Discover various methods for taking effective and organized notes during lectures or while reading textbooks.
- 💬 **Critical Thinking Skills:** Develop your ability to analyze, evaluate, and synthesize information to make informed decisions and solve problems.
- ⏰ **Time Blocking and the Pomodoro Technique:** Learn about time management techniques like time blocking and the Pomodoro Technique to enhance productivity
- 🏆 **Stress Relief Strategies:** Overcome exam anxiety with mindfulness, relaxation exercises, and mental resilience techniques.
- ▉ **Practice Makes Perfect:** Explore the importance of practice exams, sample questions, and mock tests, and understand how to analyze your performance to identify areas for improvement.
- 🍎 **Test-Taking Tactics:** Master the art of answering different types of questions, managing your time during the exam, and maintaining focus under pressure.

The following is a disclaimer of liability:

The goal of this book is to provide the reader with background information on the numerous topics that are discussed throughout the book. It is offered for sale with the understanding that neither the author nor the publisher are engaged in the practice of providing professional advice of any type, including but not limited to advice pertaining to legal matters, medical matters, or other matters. In the event that one need the aid of a professional, one must seek the assistance of an experienced professional who is qualified to provide it.

This book has been laboriously labored over in an effort to make it as accurate as is humanly feasible, and it has taken a lot of labor. However, there is a possibility that there are inaccuracies, both in the typography and the actual content of the article. The author and publisher of this book do not accept any responsibility or liability to any third party for any loss or damage caused, or represented to have been caused, directly or indirectly, by the information that is included in this book. This rule applies to any loss or harm that may have been caused, or is suspected of having been caused, by the information that is presented in this book.

This information is provided "as is," without any guarantees or warranties regarding its completeness, accuracy, usefulness, or timeliness. The information is presented "as is" without any guarantees or warranties of any kind. The reader is highly encouraged to seek the opinion of a certified expert or professionals in the field in order to obtain the most up-to-date knowledge that is currently available.

information and compiled data.

In no way, shape, or form does the viewpoints or policies of any specific organisation or professional body come over in this book in any kind whatsoever. Any slights that could be interpreted as being directed toward specific individuals or groups were not intended, despite the fact that they may have occurred.

TABLE OF CONTENT

STUDY GUIDE

Introduction

Welcome to Your MFT Exam Journey
Understanding the California MFT Licensure Process

Chapter 1: Overview of the MFT Exam

What is the California MFT Exam?
Why Passing the Exam Matters
The Structure of the Exam
Recent Changes to the Exam (2024-2025)

Chapter 2: Eligibility and Application

Eligibility Requirements
Application Process
Application Fees and Timelines
Tips for a Smooth Application

Chapter 3: Preparing for the MFT Exam

Creating a Study Plan
Recommended Study Materials
The Role of Supervision
Setting Realistic Expectations

Chapter 4: Exam Content Domains

Domain I: Theoretical Foundations and Clinical Practice
Domain II: Clinical Assessment, Diagnosis, and Treatment Planning
Domain III: Psychotherapeutic and Counseling Relationship
Domain IV: Professional Ethics, Law, Regulation, and Policies

Chapter 5: Study Strategies and Tips

Effective Study Techniques
Time Management
Balancing Work, Life, and Study
Practice Tests and Mock Exams

Chapter 6: Domain I - Theoretical Foundations and Clinical Practice

Key Concepts in Family Systems Theories
Common Clinical Approaches
Case Formulation and Treatment Planning
Sample Questions and Practice Exercises

Chapter 7: Domain II - Clinical Assessment, Diagnosis, and Treatment Planning

Diagnostic and Statistical Manual (DSM) Overview
Assessment Tools and Procedures
Developing Treatment Plans
Case Vignettes and Scenarios

Chapter 8: Domain III - Psychotherapeutic and Counseling Relationship

Building Therapeutic Alliances
Communication Skills
Multicultural Competence
Ethical Considerations in the Therapeutic Relationship

Chapter 9: Domain IV - Professional Ethics, Law, Regulation, and Policies

Legal and Ethical Framework
California Law and Regulations
Dual Relationships and Boundary Issues
Ethical Decision-Making

Chapter 10: Exam-Day Strategies

Final Week Preparation
Test-Day Checklist
Time Management During the Exam
Coping with Test Anxiety

Chapter 11: After the Exam

Receiving Your Results
Preparing for Potential Retakes
Post-Exam Licensure Requirements
Continuing Education and Professional Growth

Chapter 12: Special Topics and Emerging Trends

Cultural Competency and Diversity in Therapy
LGBTQ+ Issues in Marriage and Family Therapy
Substance Abuse and Addiction in Family Systems
Technology and Teletherapy

Chapter 13: Self-Care for Future Therapists

The Importance of Self-Care
Strategies for Maintaining Personal Well-being
Managing Compassion Fatigue
Finding Balance in Your Life and Career

Chapter 14: Case Studies and Practical Application

Real-World Case Examples
Analysis of Clinical Scenarios
Ethical Dilemmas and Solutions
Developing a Comprehensive Case Conceptualization

Chapter 15: Professional Development and Licensure Process

Understanding the Licensure Process in California
Supervision and Post-Graduate Requirements
Career Opportunities in MFT
The Role of Professional Associations

Chapter 16: Interactive Resources and Study Groups

Joining Study Groups and Online Forums
Interactive Study Apps and Tools
How to Make the Most of Online Communities
Networking for MFT Students

Chapter 17: Preparing for the California Jurisprudence Exam

Overview of the Jurisprudence Exam
Study Materials and Resources
Test Format and Content
Tips for Successful Jurisprudence Exam Preparation

Chapter 18: Staying Informed: Legal and Ethical Updates

Staying Current with Changing Laws and Regulations
Ethical Considerations in Evolving Clinical Practices
Adapting to Legal Updates in Your Practice
Resources for Ongoing Professional Development

Before we begin:

Welcome to the website for "California MFT Marriage and Family Therapy Exam Study Guide 2024-2025." In this thorough book, we set out on a path that is not only about preparing for an examination, but also about equipping you for a profession in marriage and family therapy that is both gratifying and has an impact on people's lives.

The profession of marital and family therapy is one that requires a profound comprehension of human relationships, mental health, and ethical values. While this field can be very rewarding, it can also be very demanding. Your position as an aspiring Marriage and Family Therapist (MFT) in the state of California will be critical in assisting individuals, couples, and families in navigating the intricacies of life's issues and bringing about positive change within the dynamics of their relational systems.

The procedure to become a licensed marriage and family therapist (MFT) in California is arduous, and passing the examination is one of the most important steps along the way. In order to become a licensed marriage and family therapist (MFT), you must first pass the MFT examination, which verifies that you have the knowledge and skills necessary to offer competent and compassionate therapy to your clients. This study guide is intended to serve as a resource for you as you get ready to take the Marriage and Family Therapy Exam in the state of California, which is an important step on the path to becoming a licensed therapist.

Understanding the Importance of Your Trip

The choice to pursue a career as a Marriage and Family Therapist is one that carries significant weight. It is a commitment to understanding the complexities of human relationships and emotions, as well as a dedication to the health and happiness of the people and families whose needs you will attend to. Your job as a marriage and family therapist (MFT) goes far beyond the four walls of an office; it permeates the very core of people's lives, directing them along the roads that lead to healing and self-discovery.

In order to start down this path, you will need to do well on the California MFT Exam. This test will determine whether or not you are prepared to take on the obligations that come along with holding a license to practice marriage and family therapy. Keep in mind that although it may appear to be an overwhelming chore, it is actually an opportunity for you to consolidate your information, perfect your skills, and demonstrate that you are competent. A profession in which you will truly be able to make a positive impact on the lives of the people you serve awaits you if you are successful in passing the exam.

The Heart and Soul of This Instructional Guide

This study guide will serve as your compass as you navigate the complex terrain of the California Marriage and Family Therapy Exam (MFT Marriage and Family Therapy Exam). It has been meticulously created to serve as a guide for you throughout the process, beginning with the prerequisites for eligibility and ending with the requirements for licensure after the exam. Not only do we want to ensure that you pass the exam, but we also want to set you up for a prosperous and satisfying future as a marriage and family therapist.

The Things That Are to Be Expected

In the chapters that follow, we will go into the specifics of the MFT exam, including its topic domains as well as any new modifications that have been implemented as of 2024-2025. We will go over the requirements for eligibility as well as the application process, providing you all the information and resources you will need to get started on your path toward licensing.

As we move further, we will talk about efficient methods of studying, techniques for managing one's time, and ways to strike a balance between one's personal and academic life. In addition to this, we will give you a knowledge of the four material domains that will be assessed on the exam, providing a holistic view of what is required of you as a prospective MFT.

You will discover examples of questions on the test, case studies, and activities that you can do in real life scattered throughout the guide to help you solidify your comprehension of important ideas and how to apply them. In the context of marriage and family therapy (MFT), we will also talk about professional ethics, the laws and regulations that regulate your practice, as well as the function of the therapeutic relationship.

In addition to the actual test, we cover a variety of topics that are important to your career as an MFT. These include self-care, developing trends in treatment, and maintaining awareness of the latest legal and ethical developments. We make available materials for continuous professional development, which will assist you in maintaining a practice that is both up to date and effective.

Your Development Both Personally and Professionally

Although the primary purpose of this guide is to improve your chances of passing the exam, we want to make it clear that becoming a licensed MFT requires a lifetime commitment to both personal and professional development on your part. Keep in mind that as you move forward on this journey, each step contributes to your growth as a therapist, so keep that in mind as you get started.

You will be provided with a road map by the study guide, but ultimately the voyage will be entirely up to you. Learning, self-discovery, and development are all processes that should be welcomed with open arms. Your capacity to sympathize with, comprehend, and provide help for your customers is built not only on your expertise, but also on the experiences and development you've had in your own life.

Acknowledgments and Expressions of Gratitude

The production of this study guide was a group endeavor, and I would like to express my appreciation to everyone who offered their knowledge and assistance in making this project a success. I would like to express my gratitude to the educators, mentors, and therapists who have imparted their knowledge and experience to me. Your unwavering commitment to the area of marital and family therapy serves as an excellent example.

In addition, I would like to take this opportunity to extend my gratitude to those individuals who are working toward the MFT credential and are currently on this path. I applaud your dedication to making a positive impact on the lives of other people, and I will do all in my power to help you achieve your goal of becoming a certified marriage and family therapist (MFT).

In closing, I would want to express my gratitude to the MFT candidates' families and friends. Those who are getting ready for this test are going to have a much better chance of passing if they have your steadfast support, as well as your patience and encouragement.

Closing Remarks

As you make your way through this guide, keep in mind that pursuing a career as a marriage and family therapist is an admirable goal. It is a dedication to making the world a better place one relationship at a time by prioritizing the health and happiness of individuals, as well as the stability of their families.

Introduction to the MFT Examination, Chapter 1

The path to qualifying as a Marriage and Family Therapist (MFT) in the state of California is one that is difficult to traverse but ultimately rewarding. Your ability to demonstrate that you are prepared to work in the highly specialized field of mental health that is represented by the California MFT Exam will be the deciding factor in whether or not you are successful in your endeavor. In this chapter, we will discuss the most important parts of the MFT exam, including its significance and the basis upon which your future career as a therapist will be constructed.

The Function of the MFT Examination

The Marriage and Family Therapist Exam in California is more than simply an evaluation of your knowledge and abilities; it is also a stepping stone toward a successful and meaningful career in the field of marriage and family therapy. When you become a Marriage and Family Therapist, you will be responsible for the health and happiness of individuals, couples, and families. Your job will involve addressing issues concerning mental health, interpersonal interactions, and the dynamics of the family unit. Your ability to perform these tasks in a competent, ethical, and culturally sensitive manner will be evaluated during the MFT exam, which was created to guarantee that you are well-prepared.

What exactly is the MFT Exam in the state of California?

The California MFT Exam is a standardized examination that examines your knowledge and competency in marriage and family therapy. This exam is given by the California Board of Behavioral Sciences (BBS), which is responsible for its administration. Your ability to apply theoretical concepts, carry out clinical assessments, devise treatment programs, and adhere to ethical and legal requirements will be evaluated here. In order to earn your MFT license in the state of California, one of the most important prerequisites is for you to pass this exam.

Why It Is Necessary to Do Well on the Test

In California, obtaining a license to practice as a marriage and family therapist (MFT) is not just a demonstration of your professional competency but also a legal requirement. If you do not have a current license, you will not be able to work independently as an MFT. This highlights how important it is to do well in the examination. However, passing the exam indicates that you are prepared to provide high-quality therapy services to individuals and families who seek your assistance. This is significant beyond the legal implications of the exam.

Exam Format and Organizational Principles

The format of the MFT exam is designed to test your knowledge and abilities across a wide variety of subject matter areas. The examination will include multiple-choice questions, vignettes, and constructed-response questions beginning in the 2024-2025 school year. It evaluates the following four primary content domains:

Theoretical Foundations and Clinical Practice make up the first domain, which is as follows: Your knowledge of marital and family therapy theories, clinical techniques, and your ability to apply this knowledge to real-world circumstances will be evaluated under this domain.

Assessment of the patient's condition, making a diagnosis, and planning treatment: Within the scope of this section, you will be evaluated on your ability to carry out clinical evaluations, make accurate diagnoses of mental health illnesses, and design efficient treatment programs.

Relationships in the Psychotherapeutic and Counseling Domain III: Within this domain, you will be tested on your knowledge and skills regarding the establishment and maintenance of therapeutic relationships, communication approaches, and cultural competency.

Professional Ethics, Law, and Regulations, as well as Policies and Procedures: In this sector, you will be tested on your knowledge of the ethical and legal framework within which MFTs practice, including the rules and regulations that are specific to the state of California.

Recent Modifications Made to the Test (2024-2025)

Because changes to the MFT exam can have an effect on how you choose to prepare for it, staying current on those changes is extremely important. As of the academic years 2024-2025, there have been a number of significant adjustments:

The format of the test has been updated, and it now consists of a mix of constructed-response questions, multiple-choice questions, and vignette-based questions. Your knowledge and application skills will be put through a rigorous examination thanks to the varied question types.

material Updates The California Board of Behavioral Sciences routinely evaluates and revises the exam's material in order to guarantee that it remains in step with the ever-evolving requirements of the industry. It is essential to be informed of these modifications and make preparations in accordance with them.

Score Required to Pass The minimum score required to pass the MFT exam is subject to change based on statistical analysis of the performance of candidates. Be careful to visit the BBS website for the most recent passing score, and pay close attention to any updates.

Materials for Study There may be updated study materials, test preparation tools, and practice examinations available that are geared specifically toward the changed examination format. Utilize these resources to ensure that you are appropriately prepared for whatever is ahead.

Eligibility Requirements and Application Process

The process of obtaining a marriage and family therapist (MFT) license in the state of California is one that calls for meticulous preparation, unwavering commitment, and fulfillment of a number of particular eligibility requirements. In this chapter, we will walk you through the essential processes of determining your eligibility and effectively navigating the application process so that you can apply for the position you want. Your road toward becoming an MFT in California requires that you have a foundational understanding of the requirements and complexities involved with the process.

Criteria for Acceptance into the MFT Program in the State of California

It is imperative that you determine whether or not you satisfy the eligibility requirements established by the California Board of Behavioral Sciences (BBS) in order to submit an application for the California MFT Exam. Candidates must demonstrate that they are adequately equipped to meet the obligations and ethical standards expected of certified MFTs by satisfying all of the qualifications outlined in this section. Let's have a look at the most important requirements for eligibility:

Educational Requirements: You must have graduated from an institution that is nationally or regionally accredited with a master's degree in marriage and family therapy or a field that is closely linked to this one. The prerequisites for the degree program's curriculum that have been set by the BBS must be satisfied. In most cases, this necessitates the completion of a series of predetermined classes in subjects such as marriage and family studies, individual development, and human sexuality.

You are expected to have accumulated the required number of hours of supervised experience, which usually consists of at least 3,000 hours of postgraduate supervised experience. This expertise ought to be achieved through clinical practice in the field of marital and family therapy, and it ought to be overseen by a certified mental health practitioner, preferably a registered MFT.

Coursework: In addition to having a graduate degree, you are required to have completed particular coursework in fundamental curriculum areas such human development, marriage and family systems, and professional ethics.

Clinical Experience It is important that you devote a significant percentage of your supervised experience to direct clinical work, which may include assessment, diagnosis, treatment planning, and psychotherapy services with individuals, couples, and families.

Concerning Ethical and Legal Matters: You are required to have successfully completed coursework in professional ethics as well as California law and regulations in relation to marital and family therapy.

Your supervised experience is required to involve a minimum number of hours of supervision, with a minimum number of those hours spent on an individual basis. Your continued professional growth as well as your commitment to ethical and legal norms both require that you participate in this supervision.

Application for Associate Registration Before beginning to accumulate supervised experience, you are required to submit an application with the BBS for Associate Registration. Because of this, you will be able to practice therapy under the direction of a qualified MFT. The process of registration includes a history check as well as the taking of fingerprints.

You will be required to submit to a background check and fingerprinting as part of the registration procedure. This step is necessary to ensure the safety of those who use our services. This is to guarantee that you meet the requirements for both your character and your physical fitness in order to obtain a license.

In order to be eligible to apply for the MFT Exam, you will first need to demonstrate that you have successfully completed the California Law and Ethics Exam for MFTs. This exam assesses your understanding of the legal and ethical sides of the profession, ensuring that you are well-versed in the laws and regulations that govern your practice by requiring you to demonstrate that you are familiar with both.

It is essential to keep in mind that the process of obtaining an MFT license can be difficult, and that the standards may change over time. Because of this, it is extremely important to verify the most recent requirements listed on the California BBS website or speak with a BBS representative in order to confirm that you satisfy all of the conditions that are essential.

The Procedure for Making an Application

You will be able to move on with the application process for the California MFT Exam once you have determined that you meet the requirements for the exam, as well as once you have earned your graduate degree and finished your supervised experience. This method entails the following essential stages:

Collect the Necessary Documentation Before beginning the application process, it is important to collect all of the required documentation. In most cases, this will consist of transcripts from your graduate degree program, verification of your supervised experience, certificates of completion for the relevant coursework, and evidence of your Associate Registration.

Obtaining a license in California requires the use of an online application process known as Breeze, which may be accessed through the California Board of Behavioral Sciences website. In order to access critical updates and information, in addition to submitting your application, you will be required to register a Breeze account.

Finishing the Application Form You may locate the application form for the MFT Exam inside of your Breeze account. Please include information that is both correct and up to date on this form.

Pay the Application Fee In order to take the MFT Exam, you will be required to pay an application fee, which must be done concurrently with the submission of your application. You can get the most recent version of the cost schedule on the BBS website.

Upload or submit all relevant documentation as part of your application by following the instructions in the supporting documentation section. This includes transcripts, forms verifying experience, and any other supporting materials that may be necessary.

Wait While Your Application Is Processed The BBS will review both your application and any supporting documentation that you have submitted.

Because this procedure could take some time, it is essential that you submit your application well in advance of the date that you want to take the exam.

Approval & Eligibility for the Exam: After your application has been reviewed and accepted, you will be notified of whether or not you are qualified to take the MFT Exam. This notification will include instructions on how to schedule your examination. Please read it carefully.

You are able to schedule your exam through the Pearson VUE test delivery system, which is the authorized test center for the California MFT Exam. The exam can be scheduled at a time that is convenient for you.

Get Yourself Ready for the Test: Now that you know when your test will be, it is time to develop a strategy for studying that is both targeted and efficient. You can prepare for the test with the help of the strategies and resources that are provided in this guide.

Participate in the Examination: On the day of the examination, report to the testing center well-prepared and ready to demonstrate your understanding of the material and your ability to apply it. The MFT Exam includes questions with multiple choice answers, vignettes, and constructed response questions; therefore, you need to make sure that you pace yourself appropriately.

You Will Get Your Exam Results After Completing the Exam After you have finished the exam, you will get your results. If you are successful, you will be able to move on to the subsequent stages of the licensing process. In the event that you do not achieve the required score, you will be given instructions on how to retake the examination.

Some Helpful Hints for the Application Procedure

The application procedure might be difficult to understand and navigate; thus, here are some pointers to ensure a smooth journey:

Maintain Your Organization: Make a Checklist of All Necessary Documents and Collect Them Early On Create a check list of all necessary documents and collect them early on. Check that everything is exact and complete before moving forward.

Prepare in advance: Get the application process started as soon as possible to leave room for any unforeseen delays. Because it can take the BBS some time to review applications, submitting them early increases the likelihood that you will be able to book your exam at the time of your choosing.

Be Familiar with Breeze: The Breeze web system is the major platform for applying for licensing, therefore you should become familiar with it. To simplify the process of applying for a job, you should become familiar with the features and functions of the application.

Maintaining an up-to-date knowledge base is essential because the criteria for obtaining a license and the application process may evolve over time. Make it a habit to check the BBS website on a regular basis for the latest information and changes.

During the application process, if you find that you have any uncertainties or queries, don't be afraid to contact the BBS or seek help from mentors and experienced MFTs who have already been through the procedure.

Preparing for the Marriage and Family Therapist Exam, Chapter 3

When it comes to the Marriage and Family Therapy (MFT) Exam in California, one must understand that preparation is the most important factor in determining their level of success. In this chapter, we will walk you through the essential steps of efficiently preparing for the exam so that you can feel confident on test day. This chapter will equip you with the techniques, tools, and mentality necessary for success, regardless of where you are in your journey: whether you are just starting out or have arrived at this point after satisfying the prerequisites for eligibility and completing the application procedure.

Making a Study Schedule and Plan

Developing a well-structured study plan is an absolute necessity before delving into the specifics of different types of learning methodologies. A study plan acts as a road map, enabling you to more effectively manage your time and direct your attention to the most important aspects of the material to be learned. The following steps will guide you in developing an efficient study plan:

Clearly define your objectives, such as the date of the test you intend to take and the grade you want to earn in it. Your study plan will get direction and purpose if you have a definite objective in mind.

Evaluate Your Own Capabilities and Limitations: Determine which of the four material categories of the MFT Exam—Theoretical Foundations and Clinical

Practice; Clinical Assessment, Diagnosis, and Treatment Planning; Psychotherapeutic and Counseling Relationship; and Professional Ethics, Law, Regulation, and Policies—are your strongest and weakest areas of knowledge. It is important to be aware of both the areas in which you shine and those in which you might use some development in order to make the most of the time you spend studying.

Break It Down: To make your study plan more doable, divide it up into different sections depending on the different curriculum areas. For instance, you should allot a certain amount of time to each domain based on your own evaluation of the skills and shortcomings you now possess.

Determine the number of hours that you can devote to studying on a daily or weekly basis, and set those hours accordingly. Keep a realistic perspective on the demands that your daily life places on you and your schedule.

Consider the Type of Material There are many different sorts of materials and resources available for test preparation, such as textbooks, study guides, online courses, and practice exams. You should select the type of material that best suits your needs. Think about the approach to education that suits you the most, and incorporate a variety of teaching methods into your strategy.

Include pauses: To avoid becoming burned out from studying, be sure to include time in your schedule for brief pauses. Taking frequent, little breaks will help you keep your concentration and energy levels up.

Review and Modify: At regular intervals, evaluate your current study schedule and modify it as appropriate. If you find that you are making rapid progress in one area, you might want to think about moving your attention to other areas that need more of it.

Include Time for Practice Exams in Your strategy You should make sure that your strategy includes time for you to participate in practice exams. These are quite helpful in determining whether or not you are prepared for the exam and getting you accustomed to the layout of the test.

Materials Suggested for Academic Study

You will require a variety of different study materials in order to adequately prepare for the MFT Exam. The following is a list of some of the most frequently suggested resources:

Textbooks are an outstanding example of excellent foundational resources. Textbooks in the areas of marital and family therapy, clinical assessment and diagnosis, and treatment planning are all examples. Look for readings that correspond to the several curriculum areas that will be on the test.

Study books The use of study books that are written expressly for the MFT Exam can be of tremendous assistance. They frequently simplify the subject and add questions to help students practice.

Courses Taken Online: Online courses and review programs offer structured learning, typically in the form of video lectures, practice questions, and the ability to track one's progress.

Access to Practice Exams It is essential to have access to practice exams. They allow you to evaluate your readiness and pinpoint areas in which you may make improvements because they replicate the format and content of the real exam.

Flashcards: When it comes to learning new essential terminology, definitions, and concepts, flashcards are a great tool. There are both physical and digital versions of the flashcards that can be used.

Reviewing real-world case studies and vignettes can assist you in applying your knowledge to practical circumstances, which is an essential component of the MFT Exam. Case studies and vignettes can be found here.

Supervision and Mentoring: During this stage of your preparation, it is important to seek the advice of experienced MFTs or mentors who can share insights, answer questions, and offer assistance.

Participate in Online Communities and Forums It is beneficial to take part in online communities and forums where candidates discuss their experiences and provide each other study advice. These might offer supplementary encouragement and assistance.

The Importance of Being Watched

It is impossible to overstate the importance of having a supervisor or mentor, despite the fact that self-directed study is a key component of your preparation. Seek out licensed MFTs who can offer significant insights, explain difficult topics in a way that's easy to understand, and offer advise based on their years of expertise. A mental health counselor who is already licensed can guide you through the process of getting your own license and act as a guide for you along the way.

In addition, if you have not yet finished the required number of hours of supervised experience, your clinical supervision should continue while you are preparing for the exam. Have a conversation with your supervisor about the most effective way to include knowledge related to the exam into your clinical work.

Having Expectations That Are Realistic

It is quite important to go into the process of exam preparation with reasonable expectations. The following are some crucial considerations to keep in mind:

It is more vital to maintain consistency in your study habits than to try to cram everything in at the last minute. Make learning a consistent component of your day-to-day activities and routines.

Learning and retaining the information necessary for the MFT Exam is a process that takes time. Progress must be patiently anticipated. Take it easy on yourself and try to avoid putting undue stress on yourself.

You'll feel more at ease with both the structure and the material if you complete more practice questions and tests. The more of these you do, the more proficient you'll become.

Recognize that life will go on even as you are preparing for the test, and do your best to strike a balance between the two. The key to long-term success is striking a healthy balance between one's academic pursuits and their personal lives.

Taking Action to Improve Weak Areas It's natural to have some areas in which you feel less secure than others. Devote more time and effort to correcting these flaws, seeking assistance and more resources if necessary.

Take Care of Yourself: It's important to remember to take care of yourself. During this time of intense preparation, it is really necessary to take care of both your physical and mental health.

Methods of Approaching Tests

As the date of your test draws closer, you should give some thought to the following test-taking strategies:

Read the Instructions Before going into the questions, it is important to make sure you have a thorough understanding of the format and organization of the exam by reading the instructions first.

Because there is a time limit on the MFT Exam, it is important that you budget your time properly. Do not allow yourself to become trapped on difficult questions; instead, move on and come back to them if there is time.

Remember that there is no penalty for making educated guesses, therefore it is imperative that you answer each and every question. If you are unsure of something, you should make an educated assumption.

Make the Most of Your Break: You will most likely be given a break throughout the MFT Exam. Make the most of this time to get some rest, concentrate, and recharge your energy.

If you finish the test with time to spare, go back over your answers and make sure everything is correct. If you don't feel comfortable with the modifications you want to make, proceed with caution.

Maintain your composure; although test anxiety is very frequent, it is manageable. Maintain your composure, take several slow, deep breaths, and direct your attention to the problem at issue.

Tests of Proficiency and Mock Examinations

Participating in practice examinations and simulated tests is an essential component of your preparation. These evaluations are useful for a variety of critical objectives, including the following:

Familiarization: Taking practice exams will help you become accustomed to the layout, structure, and different types of questions that will be on the actual examination.

Mastery of the Content: They test both your knowledge and your understanding of the content, and then they assist you identify areas in which you need additional study.

Time Management: In order to ensure that you are able to finish the exam within the specified amount of time, practice exams provide you the opportunity to practice time management and pacing.

Stress Reduction: The more practice exams you take, the more at ease you'll get with the actual process of taking tests as a result of doing so. This can help lessen anxiety on the day of the test.

Evaluation of Performance: Analyzing how well you did on practice tests will help you identify areas in which you shine and those in which you could use some work.

Additional Methods of Learning to Consider

In addition to taking mock exams, the following other studying tactics will assist you in efficiently preparing for the real thing:

Participate actively in the learning process by interacting directly with the content. Create your own personal summaries of important ideas, draw mental maps, and then demonstrate your understanding of the content to another person. Active learning increases one's ability to retain information.

Research has shown that studying in a group can be advantageous since it allows participants to discuss difficult ideas, provide encouragement and incentive to one another, and answer each other's concerns. However, you should make sure that the group continues to concentrate on studying.

Reviewing Previously Covered content on a Regular Basis: Reviewing previously covered content on a regular basis helps to enhance your understanding and sustain your recall.

Mnemonic Devices When trying to remember difficult ideas, lists, or theories, mnemonic devices, acronyms, and other memory aides can be quite helpful.

Utilize Technology: Make use of technology by utilizing resources such as flashcard apps, interactive study materials, and online discussion forums.

Exam Content Domains, Section 4, Chapter 4

The Marriage and Family Therapy (MFT) Exam in California is intended to test your level of expertise and knowledge in a variety of content areas that are essential for working in the field of marriage and family therapy in the state of California. In order to effectively prepare for the exam, it is vital to have a solid understanding of the material domains and the competencies associated with them. We will delve into the four content domains that make up the MFT Exam in this chapter, giving you with an in-depth overview of what each domain entails and the abilities that are necessary to flourish in them.

Theoretical Groundwork and Practical Experience make up the First Domain.

The First Domain: An Introduction

The MFT profession is built on the foundation of Domain I. The theoretical foundations and practical applications of giving therapy to individuals, couples, and families are the primary topics covered in this course. In this domain, you will be evaluated on how successfully you can integrate marital and family therapy theories and clinical procedures in practice.

Important Capabilities

Theoretical Foundations: This competency evaluates your knowledge of a variety of marriage and family therapy theories, including but not limited to Bowenian, Structural, Strategic, Narrative, and Systemic theories. Your knowledge of these theories will be used to determine whether or not you have met the requirements for this competency. You need to be able to recognize the most important ideas, guiding principles, and practical implementations of these theories when applied in a clinical environment.

Assessment and Diagnosis: If you want to be successful in this competency, you need to have a solid understanding of the process of assessing and diagnosing clients, which includes both individual and relationship assessments. You need to be able to recognize and differentiate between the many different concerns relating to mental health and disorders that can occur within family systems.

Case Formulation and Treatment Planning: This skill examines your ability to conceptualize a complete case based on the information acquired during evaluations in order to plan appropriate treatments for the patient. You should be experienced in designing suitable treatment plans that address the specific requirements of individuals, couples, and families. This includes the ability to tailor treatment to meet the needs of multiple generations within a family.

Cultural Competence: It is essential to have a solid understanding of the cultural elements that can impact treatment. This competency evaluates your capacity to work productively with a wide variety of client populations, requiring you to demonstrate cultural sensitivity while also adjusting your therapeutic approach to meet the needs of each client group.

Family Dynamics and Systems Thinking: You should be proficient in recognizing and analyzing family dynamics, roles, and interactions within a systemic framework. This requires that you have the ability to think in a systemic way. This includes having an awareness of how a shift in the behavior of a single family member can influence the dynamics of the whole system.

Clinical procedures: This competency will evaluate how well you are able to implement clinical procedures, interventions, and strategies. This includes your capacity to create good change within family structures, as well as to settle conflicts, facilitate communication, and resolve disagreements.

Ethical and Legal Considerations The ethical and legal standards that direct the practice of MFT are an essential part of this field. You have a responsibility to educate yourself on the moral standards and legal requirements that are associated with the profession.

Research and Evaluation: In order to demonstrate this ability, you will need to demonstrate a comprehension of research methodology and evaluation procedures. It is expected of you to be able to make use of research in order to improve and inform your clinical practice.

Clinical evaluation, medical diagnosis, and treatment planning make up the second domain.

Introduction to the Second Domain

Assessment, diagnosis, and the planning of treatment are some of the topics that are covered in Domain II, which focuses on the most important aspects of clinical practice. These are the key skills that marriage and family therapists (MFTs) need to possess in order to give effective therapy to their clients. Your competence to conduct clinical evaluations, identify mental health issues, and design thorough treatment programs will be evaluated in this domain.

Important Capabilities

procedures of Assessment: If you want to do well in this competency, you need to be familiar with the many different types of assessment procedures and tools that are utilized in clinical practice. This includes the capacity to interview clients and their families, as well as the ability to give standardized tests and collect pertinent information from clients and their families.

You should be adept at gathering and evaluating information regarding the client's past as well as the issues that are now being presented to you. This involves the capacity to analyze the influence on the client's well-being of the dynamics at play in the client's family, relationships, and the surrounding environment.

Diagnostic Skills Comprehension of a variety of mental health conditions and the ability to differentiate between them are essential components of this talent. The Diagnostic and Statistical Manual (DSM) contains the criteria that must be met in order for you to be able to provide an appropriate diagnosis of a client's condition.

Assessment of Biopsychosocial Factors It is essential to carry out exhaustive assessments of the client's biopsychosocial factors in order to grasp the complexities of the client's mental health and relational problems. This involves addressing the client's biological, psychological, and social variables, all of which contribute to the client's overall well-being.

The process of formulating treatment plans requires you to have expertise in establishing tailored treatment plans based on the findings of the assessment and the requirements of the client. This entails the establishment of objectives, the selection of suitable actions, and the ongoing assessment and modification of the plan in accordance with evolving requirements.

Communication and Collaboration: One of the most important aspects of this competency is the ability to communicate effectively with other medical professionals and collaborate with them when appropriate. In order to conduct successful evaluations and treatments, it is essential to maintain open lines of communication with the patients, their families, and the other members of the healthcare team.

Intervention in Crises: Being ready to deal with unexpected problems and catastrophes is an essential aspect of this ability. This includes possessing the abilities necessary to recognize problems that require immediate attention and to intervene in those situations.

Cultural Sensitivity: Cultural Competence is also an essential part of this domain. You should be able to perform evaluations and establish treatment plans that are sensitive to different cultures and can be adapted to meet the specific requirements of clients who come from a variety of backgrounds.

Relationships of a Psychotherapeutic and Counseling Nature (Domain III)

An Explanation of the Third Domain

Relationships, both psychological and counseling, are the focus of work done in Domain III. It examines your ability to form and sustain therapeutic partnerships, as well as your ability to exercise cultural competency, communicate successfully with clients, and effectively engage with other professionals. Establishing a solid therapeutic relationship is necessary in order to achieve positive results from treatment.

Important Capabilities

Establishing Therapeutic Alliances: The Establishing Therapeutic Alliances skill evaluates your ability to form robust therapeutic alliances with clients. You should be excellent at creating a safe space that is compassionate and nonjudgmental for clients, so that they feel comfortable discussing their ideas and feelings in your presence.

Communication with Empathy The ability to communicate effectively is one of the most important aspects of this subject. You should be able to engage in active listening, provide responses based on empathy, and facilitate open and honest discussion with customers.

The ability to communicate effectively with people of different cultures is essential to possessing multicultural competence. You should be able to work with customers who come from a variety of cultural backgrounds while simultaneously appreciating and respecting the distinctive views, values, and experiences of each individual customer.

Client-Centered Therapy: In this competency, your ability to execute client-centered therapeutic techniques including Person-Centered Therapy and Narrative Therapy will be examined.

Active Engagement and Participation: You should have a good handle on actively involving clients in the therapeutic process, encouraging their active participation, and assisting them in establishing and achieving their therapeutic goals.

Management of Boundaries: An essential component of this competency is the ability to maintain professional boundaries. It is important for you to have a solid understanding of the moral principles that control the bounds of the therapeutic interaction.

Resolving Challenges It is essential to be able to recognize and work through difficulties that may arise within the therapy partnership. This includes efficiently managing challenges relating to transference and countertransference, as well as conflicts and resistance.

Evaluation of Progress: Evaluating the development of a patient's condition and determining whether or not modifications to the treatment strategy are required are both components of this ability. This involves doing an analysis of how effective the interventions are and adapting them as required.

Professional Ethics, Law, Regulation, and Policy are Included in the Fourth Domain.

Introduction to the Fourth Domain

The ethical, legal, and regulatory concerns that arise from working as an MFT in the state of California are the primary focus of Domain IV. Your knowledge of professional ethics, the laws that govern your practice, and the specific regulations that are applicable to MFTs in the state will be evaluated as part of this process.

Important Capabilities

Legal and Ethical Standards: Your knowledge of the rules and regulations that regulate the practice of MFT in California will be evaluated based on your performance in this competency. This includes having a working knowledge of the California Business and Professions Code as well as the California Code of Regulations.

Privacy and Confidentiality: You should be familiar about the various legal and ethical requirements for safeguarding the privacy and confidentiality of client information in accordance with professional standards. This ability requires a knowledge of the many exemptions to the rule of secrecy.

Informed Consent It is important that you are able to gain informed consent from your clients and that you are able to do it in a way that ensures your clients understand the nature and purpose of therapy, as well as the potential risks and benefits, and their rights as clients.

Dual Relationships: Being able to comprehend and effectively manage dual relationships is an essential component of this competency. You should be able to recognize and address the possibility of boundary violations and conflicts of interest as well as other potential issues.

Reporting Abuse to Authorities is a Part of This ability It is a part of this ability to be aware of the legal requirements for reporting child abuse and neglect. You need to be aware of when and how to report incidents of this nature.

Documentation and Records Relating to Clients It is crucial that you have the ability to keep documentation and records relating to clients that are accurate and complete. This includes having a thorough awareness of the appropriate paperwork for assessment, diagnosis, treatment planning, and progress notes.

You need to be familiar with the scope of practice for MFTs in California, which includes the restrictions placed on your ability to practice as well as the types of services that you are permitted to render.

Professional Liability: Comprehending the significance of carrying professional liability insurance and being aware of how it connects to your work is an essential component of this skill.

Making Decisions Based on Ethics: Your ability to successfully make ethical decisions and address ethical challenges will be evaluated based on your performance in this competency. You ought to be able to apply ethical principles to events that occur in the real world.

Strategies That Will Prove Useful During Your Preparation for the MFT Exam

You need to have a full understanding of the material domains and the accompanying competencies in order to be successful on the MFT Exam. The following are some ways for good preparation:

Review of the Content Do a comprehensive review of each content domain and the associated competencies with it. Find the areas in which you have the least amount of self-assurance and devote more of your study time to improving those areas.

Practice Questions You should give yourself practice tests and answer practice questions that cover all of the relevant competencies. This will assist you with applying what you have learned and evaluating how well prepared you are.

Study Groups: Think about being a part of an existing study group, or starting one of your own, so that you may talk about the many content domains, share your thoughts, and answer each other's questions.

Supervision and Mentoring Seek out the guidance and supervision of MFTs who have more experience. They are able to supply insightful information regarding the subject domains and the competencies.

Ethical Conundrums One of the finest ways to practice ethical decision-making is to examine ethical conundrums and think carefully about the best way to proceed.

Case Studies: In order to demonstrate your ability to apply what you've learned to real-world situations, which is a significant component of the test, you'll need to work with case studies and vignettes.

Maintain Accurate Knowledge: Ensure that you maintain accurate knowledge of the ever-changing rules, regulations, and ethical requirements that pertain to MFT practice in the state of California.

When taking practice examinations, it is important to work on your time management skills in order to ensure that you will be able to finish the real exam within the allotted amount of time.

Review Your Performance on Practice tests and Ask for Feedback You should review your performance on practice tests and ask for feedback from mentors and peers in order to find areas in which you may improve.

Self-Care: It is important to remember to take care of yourself. During this time of intense preparation, it is really necessary to take care of both your physical and mental health.

Chapter 5: Methods and Suggestions for Academic Success

Successfully passing the California Marriage and Family Therapy (MFT) Exam is contingent on your utilization of efficient study methods. The preparation for this complex exam calls for undivided attention, meticulous organization, and a methodical strategy. In this chapter, we will discuss a variety of approaches to studying and provide helpful hints in order to assist you in making the most of your preparation and improving your chances of passing the MFT Exam.

1. Establish a Regular and Organized Study Routine

The foundation of efficient test preparation is a study program that is well-structured and organized. When planning your study routine, keep the following suggestions in mind:

Establish concrete study objectives, such as the completion of a predetermined number of practice questions or the traversal of a given content domain.

Create in your daily or weekly plan specific blocks of time that are solely devoted to learning.

Maintaining a routine when you study will help you develop a habit that will eventually feel like second nature.

Make a visual study schedule for yourself so that you can keep track of your progress and be accountable to yourself.

Include time for breaks and leisure activities in your schedule to protect yourself from burnout and keep your motivation up.

2. Get a Head Start

It is critical to start preparations in advance. When you have more time to study, you will be better able to cover all of the extensive material domains and practice enough to be successful. Avoid putting things off till the last minute and start preparing for your exam as soon as possible.

3. Establish Specific Objectives

Establish clear and attainable objectives for each of your study sessions. These objectives could be based on content domains, the amount of practice questions to be solved, or certain subject areas to be mastered. Having well-defined goals not only helps you keep your attention on the task at hand but also allows you to track your progress.

4. Make Use of a Wide Range of Resources 4.

Don't put all of your faith into a single category of learning resources. Combine different types of resources, such as textbooks, study guides, online courses, practice examinations, flashcards, and case studies. Mix and match the resources. The use of a variety of resources enables students to have exposure to a wide range of perspectives and educational possibilities.

5. Participatory Instruction

Take an active interest in the content to be studied. Do something more active than reading, such as creating mind maps, summarizing significant concepts in your own words, or explaining the material to another person. Learning that is more active improves both understanding and retention.

6. Prepare yourself by taking sample tests.

Participating in some practice examinations is an essential component of your preparation. You will be able to determine whether or not you are prepared for the real MFT Exam by taking these exams, which replicate the structure and content of the real exam. Be sure to give yourself practice exams in an environment that is similar to the real test, paying attention to the clock and avoiding distractions.

7. Conducting Routine Audits

Reviewing content you've already learned on a regular basis will help you better understand it and keep more of it in your memory. When it comes to remembering information over a longer period of time, the strategy of spaced repetition, in which material is reviewed at increasing intervals, can be very effective.

8. Seek Advice and Assistance from Older People.

Seek the advice of experienced MFTs or mentors if you have access to either of these resources. They are able to offer useful insights, make complex subjects easier to understand, and provide direction based on their years of expertise. During the course of your preparation, mentoring can be a very helpful resource.

9. Discussion Groups

Take into consideration participating in or organizing a study group with other applicants. You will be able to provide each other with encouragement and inspiration while studying together, as well as discuss difficult ideas and answer each other's questions. However, you should make sure that the group keeps its attention on the subject at hand.

10. Focus on Improving Your Weak Points

Determine the areas in which you need more work and devote more of your study time to improving those areas. If you want to strengthen your understanding in these areas, look for further materials or get some advice. It is essential to ensure that you have a comprehensive understanding of all content domains in order to be successful.

11. Recreate the Conditions of the Exam

When you are doing practice tests, you should try to recreate the conditions of the real test. Place yourself in a calm and peaceful space, strictly adhere to the allotted amount of time, and make use of the same resources as you will on the actual exam. This will assist you in becoming more familiar with the layout of the examination room.

12. Ensure That You Are Up-to-Date With Any Changes

There is a possibility that both the content and format of the MFT Exam will evolve over time. Checking the website of the California Board of Behavioral Sciences (BBS) on a frequent basis or speaking with a BBS representative are both great ways to ensure that you are up to date on any modifications or additions that have been made to the test.

13. Methods for Making Ethical Decisions in Practice

Consider the various options available when faced with a moral conundrum and develop your ability to make ethical decisions by doing so. On the MFT Exam, you will frequently be asked to respond to ethical issues, so it is necessary to have a solid ethical basis.

14. Maintain both your physical and mental well-being.

Ensure that both your physical and emotional health are in good shape. Check that you are receiving enough sleep, that you are exercising regularly, and that you are eating in a healthy way. Your efforts in school will benefit substantially from the mental clarity and physical vitality that come with leading a healthy lifestyle.

15. Learn to Overcome Your Test Anxiety

Anxiety before exams is rather normal, but it can be controlled. Before the test, try calming activities like meditation or deep breathing to settle your anxiety and prepare yourself mentally. In addition, practice positive self-talk and regularly remind yourself of the things you've accomplished and how prepared you are.

16. Prioritize Being Consistent Over Cramming

Cramming is not as effective as maintaining a routine study schedule that is consistent. Instead of depending on rigorous study sessions at the last minute, make studying a regular part of your day-to-day routine instead.

17. Focus on Improving Your Weaknesses, Too

Even while it's crucial to work on improving your weaknesses, you shouldn't ignore your strong points. Make it a priority to maintain your stellar performance in the content areas in which you are already well-versed.

18. Maintain a Happy and Confident Attitude

Have faith in yourself and the skills you possess. Your performance on the test can be significantly improved by adopting a constructive mental attitude and having faith in the effectiveness of your preparation.

19. Evaluate Your Own Progression

Maintain a regular schedule of self-evaluation. It is possible to accomplish this goal by engaging in self-evaluation or by participating in mock examinations. Adjust your study plan based on the findings of your assessment and put more emphasis on the topics that require more work.

20. Make Your Study Space As Comfortable As Possible

Create an atmosphere that is conducive to learning. Make sure you have everything you need, including a peaceful space to study, as few distractions as possible, and all of the required supplies. Make sure you have a place that is conducive to production and concentration.

21. Maintain a Current Knowledge of the Law and Ethical Standards

It is possible for laws and ethical standards to evolve throughout time. Maintain a level of familiarity with the most up-to-date legal and ethical standards that govern the practice of MFT in the state of California.

22. Seek Assistance from Your Close Friends and Family

Inform your loved ones and close friends about the preparations you are making for the exam. They are able to offer emotional support and assist in the creation of an environment that is suitable to study by respecting your study time and space.

23. Strive to Achieve a Healthy Work–Life Balance

Try to keep in mind that life will go on even when you are studying for the exam. The key to long-term success is striking a healthy balance between one's academic pursuits and their personal lives. Try not to stress yourself out with too much schoolwork and ignore other important parts of your life.

24. Address Your Concerns About Taking Tests

Anxiety about taking a test is very normal, and it can have a detrimental effect on your performance. To combat this, engage in relaxation practices such as deep breathing and mindfulness, and give some thought to enlisting the assistance of a therapist or counselor if you find that worry is seriously impacting the quality of your performance.

25. Evaluate Responses That Are Not Correct

Pay particular attention to the questions on the practice tests that you answered wrong when you go back to review them. Consider why you got the answers wrong and work on enhancing your comprehension in the relevant subject areas.

Domain I: Theoretical Foundations and Clinical Practice, which is covered in Chapter 6

The Marriage and Family Therapy (MFT) Exam in California focuses on the most important aspects of the profession in its Domain I. It places its primary emphasis on the theoretical underpinnings and practical applications that serve as the cornerstone of marriage and family therapy. In the following chapter, we will go deeper into the intricacies of Domain I, giving you with a full grasp of the theoretical frameworks and clinical practices that are fundamental to this domain.

the theoretical underpinnings

The theoretical underpinnings of a treatment are essential to its overall success. They offer a framework for comprehending human behavior as well as the dynamics of family life and interpersonal interactions. Your knowledge of the many MFT theories, their central principles, and their applications in clinical practice will be evaluated as part of the Domain I portion of the exam.

1. The Bowenian Theory of the Family System

The Bowenian theory places a strong emphasis on the concept of self-differentiation, as well as emotional triangles, family systems, and the influence that multi-generational family dynamics have on individuals.

Application in Clinical Practice: Therapists who adhere to Bowenian theory frequently assist clients in understanding their family systems, becoming more self-aware, and reducing emotional reactivity in relationships.

2. Family Therapy With a Structural Focus

The concepts of family organization, boundaries, and hierarchies are the primary areas of attention in structural therapy. It analyzes unhealthy family structures and works to remodel them so that healthier relationships can be achieved.

Application in Clinical Work: Structural therapists actively engage with families to reorganize the ways in which family members interact with one another in order to develop more adaptable family systems.

3. Family Therapy Utilizing a Strategic Approach

Concepts Fundamental to the Field Problem-solving, communication patterns, and the potency of paradox are emphasized heavily in strategic therapy. It frequently makes use of strategic interventions in order to break up dysfunctional family dynamics.

Clinical Application: Counselors working with families to alter their patterns of communication and approaches to problem-solving in order to strengthen their relationships with one another through the use of strategic therapy.

4. Therapeutic Use of Narratives

The stories that people tell about their life are at the center of narrative therapy's treatment approach. Clients are assisted in reframing their narratives, with an emphasis placed on their strengths and ability to bounce back.

Narrative therapists help their clients rewrite their life stories to foster personal growth and resilience. This is one of the clinical applications of narrative therapy.

5. Treatment of the Whole System

Principal Ideas: Systemic therapy examines clients in the context of their social environments, taking into account the ways in which relationships and systems affect both behavior and overall health.

Clinical Application: Systemic therapists investigate how clients' relational patterns influence them and then collaborate with their patients to develop healthier dynamics.

Evaluation of the Patient

The process of obtaining information about clients, their current problems, and the dynamics of their families is referred to as clinical assessment. Your competence to conduct assessments, identify mental health issues, and design comprehensive treatment plans will be evaluated in Domain I of the exam.

1. Techniques for Evaluating

Interviews, standardized tests, and the gathering of pertinent information from clients and their families are all examples of approaches that can be utilized throughout the evaluation process.

Clinical Application: Therapists make use of assessment methodologies in order to gain a better understanding of the client's background, the presenting problems, and the family dynamics involved.

2. Background information on the client and current problems

The evaluation of a client's past and current concerns requires an awareness of the client's background, the reason the client is seeking treatment, and the impact that family dynamics have on the client's well-being.

In clinical practice, therapists look into the client's personal and family history to see what aspects of the client's life may be contributing to their problems.

3. Capabilities in Diagnosis

The capacity to accurately diagnose mental health illnesses based on criteria specified in the Diagnostic and Statistical Manual (DSM) is an essential part of having diagnostic abilities.

The clinical use of diagnostic skills involves the determination of therapists as to whether or not a patient satisfies the criteria for a certain mental health issue.

4. Evaluation of the Biopsychosocial Factors

The key concepts to keep in mind are that a biopsychosocial assessment takes into account the biological, psychological, and social variables that contribute to the well-being of a client.

Clinical Application Therapists conduct biopsychosocial evaluations in order to acquire a holistic understanding of the client's situation.

5. Developing Plans for Patient Treatment

The information that is acquired during assessments is used to establish treatment programs for patients. They decide on goals, choose therapies, and devise a strategy for the progression of the therapeutic process.

Clinical application: Therapists collaborate with their clients to develop tailored treatment programs that take into account the clients' particular requirements and objectives.

6. Working Together and Talking to Each Other

The ability to effectively communicate with clients, their families, and other members of the healthcare team, as well as collaborate with other medical experts, is vital for the proper assessment and treatment of patients.

In clinical practice, it is expected of therapists to communicate in a straightforward and honest manner with their patients and to work together with other medical experts as needed.

7. Responding to Emergencies

Key Concepts: The ability to intervene in crisis situations is absolutely necessary in order to deal with urgent high-risk situations that demand quick attention.

Clinical application: When clients or their families are experiencing a crisis, therapists analyze the situation and intervene, offering the essential assistance and resources that are required.

8. sensitivity to different cultures

It is essential to have cultural competency when conducting assessments in order to guarantee that patients hailing from a wide variety of cultural backgrounds receive care that is both sensitive and appropriate.

Clinical Application Therapists modify their evaluation procedures so that they are more culturally sensitive, taking into account the specific requirements of a different clientele.

The formulation of the case and the planning of the treatment

Following the completion of the assessment, the next step for the therapist is to formulate the case and design the treatment. This involves putting together a complete case conceptualization and treatment plan by combining the findings of the evaluation.

1. The Construction of the Case

The creation of a full grasp of the client's issues, family dynamics, and the elements contributing to their worries is required for the development of a case.

Clinical Application: Therapists utilize case formulation as a guide to help them grasp the circumstances of the client, which ensures that they have a complete view of the client's issues.

2. The Planning of Treatment

The formulation of precise, measurable, achievable, relevant, and time-bound (SMART) goals, the selection of appropriate interventions, and the sketching of a plan for achieving therapeutic success are all essential components of treatment planning.

Clinical Application: Therapists work closely with their clients to develop treatment plans that take into account the clients' individual requirements and lay out a course of action for the client's future therapeutic growth.

Competence Across Cultures

Domain I's importance can't be overstated, especially when it comes to cultural competency. It is essential to efficient practice to have a solid understanding of the role that cultural influences play in treatment.

1. Capacity for Intercultural Communication

Concepts Crucial to Understanding Understanding and respecting the distinct ideas, values, and experiences of customers who come from a variety of cultural backgrounds is an essential component of multicultural competency.

Clinical Application: Therapists work to create a therapy environment that is culturally sensitive and adjust their therapies to fit the individual requirements of clients who come from a wide variety of backgrounds.

2. The Dynamics of the Family and Thinking in Systems

It is essential for MFTs to have a solid grasp of family dynamics as well as systemic thinking. Your ability to detect and interpret family dynamics and roles within a systemic framework will be evaluated as part of Domain I of the Family Systems Competency Exam.

1. The dynamics of the family

The relationships, roles, and patterns of communication that occur within a family system are all a part of what psychologists refer to as "family dynamics."

Clinical Application: Therapists evaluate the dynamics of the client's family in order to gain a better understanding of how those dynamics contribute to the client's presenting problems and then utilize this understanding to influence therapeutic strategies.

2. Thinking in terms of systems

Important Ideas Realizing that a single member's behavior can influence the dynamics of the entire family unit is an essential part of practicing systems thinking.

Clinical application: Therapists collaborate with families to identify and address the impact of individual changes on the dynamic of the family, with the goal of fostering stronger relationships among family members.

Methods Used in Clinical Settings

In Domain I, having a high level of expertise in the application of clinical procedures, interventions, and strategies is absolutely necessary. This involves the ability to promote positive change within family structures, as well as to settle conflicts, enhance communication, and encourage positive change.

1. Methods Used in Clinical Settings

The concepts that are essential to understand are as follows: clinical approaches include a variety of interventions that try to promote positive change within family systems, facilitate communication, and resolve disputes.

Clinical Application: Therapists employ clinical procedures in order to treat particular problems and encourage healthy family dynamics.

2. Factors to Consider From a Moral and Legal Standpoint

In the field of marriage and family therapy (MFT), adhering to ethical and legal standards is essential. Your understanding of the ethical principles and legal requirements that are pertinent to the profession will be evaluated in Domain I of the exam.

1. Fundamental Values and Beliefs

The concepts of informed consent, confidentiality, and professional boundaries are some examples of the key concepts that are included in ethical principles.

Clinical Application: Therapists ensure that the rights of their clients are respected and that ethical norms are followed by adhering to ethical principles in their practices.

2. Considerations from a Legal Standpoint

The laws and regulations that govern the practice of MFT in California need to be comprehended in order to properly address the legal aspects of the situation.

Clinical Application: Therapists ensure that they are in conformity with legal standards by adhering to the rules and regulations that regulate their practice.

3. Conducting Studies and Analyses

In order to pass Domain I, you need to demonstrate that you have an awareness of research methodology and evaluation processes. Utilizing research in order to improve and inform clinical practice is part of this process.

1. Techniques for Conducting Research

Principal Ideas: The term "research methodologies" refers to a wide range of approaches to the process of conducting research, including both qualitative and quantitative procedures.

Clinical application refers to the process by which therapists can use the findings of research to inform their practice and keep themselves apprised of the most recent advancements in their area.

2. The Processes of Evaluation

The evaluation process involves determining how beneficial various treatment methods are and acting on that information based on your findings.

Clinical Application: Therapists make use of evaluation techniques in order to gauge the development that their clients are making and to make required alterations to their treatment programs.

Tips for Achieving Success in the First Domain: Clinical Practice and Theoretical Foundations

Now that you have a thorough comprehension of Domain I, I will share some pointers with you that will help you flourish in this domain:

1. Evaluate the Existing Theoretical Frameworks

Invest some time in conducting a thorough analysis of the primary theoretical frameworks covered in Domain I. Be sure that you are able to recognize essential concepts and the clinical uses of those notions. You might find it useful to construct flashcards or summary notes for each of the different theories.

2. The Formulation of Practice Cases

Formulate hypothetical cases in order to gain experience in case formulation. Develop your capacity to generate detailed case conceptualizations and to synthesize the findings of assessments you've conducted.

3. Place an emphasis on being culturally competent

Culture sensitivity should be given careful consideration. Acquaint yourself with the cultural aspects that can have an effect on treatment, and practice changing your approach to meet the specific requirements of clients who come from a variety of backgrounds.

4. Demonstrate an Awareness of the Legal and Ethical Standards

Be sure that you have a solid comprehension of the ethical concepts and legal standards that are applicable to your line of work. Maintain a level of awareness of the most recent changes to the applicable rules and regulations.

5. Make Use of Different Clinical Techniques

It is important to put into practice therapeutic strategies and interventions that will help to improve communication, bring about the resolution of conflicts, and encourage positive transformation within family systems. Playing roles and participating in exercises based on simulated situations might be beneficial.

6. Educate yourself on research and assessment methods.

Get yourself acquainted with the various research methodologies and analysis procedures. Prepare yourself to incorporate the findings of research into your therapeutic work in order to improve it.

7. Seek Guidance and Direction from Experienced Individuals

You could want to look into getting supervision or guidance from more experienced MFTs. They are able to offer helpful advice, share insights gained from practical experience, and provide direction about the application of theory to clinical practice.

8. Methods for Making Ethical Decisions in Practice

Participate in ethical decision-making activities to improve your capacity to handle ethical conundrums that may crop up in clinical practice.

9. Keep abreast on the Most Recent Theories

Maintain a state of current awareness of the most recent advancements in MFT ideas and practices. Maintaining an up-to-date knowledge base is vital to your success in the field of treatment, which is constantly undergoing change.

10. Practices that Promote Health and Well-Being

Take care of yourself first and foremost. During this time of intensive preparation, it is absolutely essential to take care of both your physical and mental health. You will be better prepared for the challenges of the test if both your mind and body are in good health.

Domain II (Clinical Assessment, Diagnosis, and Treatment Planning), which is covered in Chapter 7

Assessment, diagnosis, and treatment planning are three of the most important components of clinical practice, and Domain II of the California Marriage and Family Therapy (MFT) Exam is devoted to testing candidates' knowledge of these topics. In this chapter, we will delve into the specifics of Domain II in order to provide you with an in-depth comprehension of these essential aspects of MFT practice.

Techniques of Evaluation

In the field of marriage and family therapy, assessment procedures are an essential component of clinical treatment. They are the first step in gaining an insight of the client's worries, the dynamics of the client's family, and the elements that contribute to the client's well-being. In Domain II, both your knowledge and your ability to apply a variety of evaluation strategies will be analyzed and scored.

1. Interrogatories

Interviews are a method for gathering information about a client's concerns, background, and the dynamics of their family through the use of direct interactions with the client. These discussions may be completely unstructured or partially structured.

The clinical use of interviews is that they allow therapists to build rapport with clients and acquire insights into the unique experiences and difficulties faced by each individual patient.

2. Evaluations that are standardized

Important Ideas Standardized assessments are established and validated instruments that are used to measure particular components of a client's mental and emotional well-being, family dynamics, or relationship functioning. They can also be used to examine how well a family or relationship is operating.

Clinical Application: Therapists can utilize standardized evaluations to acquire measurable data about a client's condition and enhance their own clinical judgment.

3. Instruments for Evaluating the Family

Concepts Essential to Understanding Family Assessment techniques are developed to examine the functioning, relationships, and dynamics of families. The use of these techniques can assist therapists in identifying problems that exist within the context of the family.

Clinical Application: Therapists evaluate family dynamics and relationships with the help of family assessment instruments, which guides their understanding of the client's situation.

4. Ecomaps and Genograms of the Area

Both genograms and ecomaps are graphical depictions of a client's family structure, as well as their ties with one another and their wider social connections. They present a brief summary of the client's overall ecosystem.

The clinical use of genograms and ecomaps involves the visual mapping of familial links, important life events, and support networks.

Client Background and Currently Existing Concerns

It is essential for an MFT practitioner to have a solid grasp of both the past of their client and the problems that they currently face. In Domain II, you will be evaluated based on your ability to collect thorough client histories and appraise the client's current concerns. This competence is essential for the role.

1. Background on the Customer

The collection of a client's history entails the gathering of information regarding the client's personal history, family history, significant life events, and previous therapy experiences.

Clinical Application: Therapists use client histories to better understand their patients' contexts, personal experiences, and how their family histories have influenced them.

2. The Problems That Are Present

The problems, concerns, or symptoms that a client is experiencing at the time of their initial therapy session are referred to as their "presenting issues." To construct a precise clinical picture, it is necessary to have a solid understanding of these concerns.

Clinical application: therapists determine the nature of the presenting problems and the influence those problems have on the client's well-being and the dynamic of their family.

Competences in Diagnosis

The diagnosis of mental health issues is an essential component of the work that MFTs do. Your capacity to correctly diagnose clients based on criteria listed in the Diagnostic and Statistical Manual (DSM) will be examined in Domain II of the exam.

1. The Criteria of the DSM

The Diagnostic and Statistical Manual of Mental illnesses (DSM) contains diagnostic criteria as well as categories for mental health illnesses. It provides instructions for diagnosing particular illnesses and disorders in a patient.

Clinical Application Counselors consult the DSM criteria for determining whether or not their clients have the characteristics associated with a particular mental health disorder.

2. The Process of Differential Diagnosis

The process of differentiating between disorders of similar nature in the client's mental health based on the client's symptoms and medical history is known as differential diagnosis.

In clinical practice, therapists employ a method called differential diagnosis to arrive at the most accurate diagnosis possible by first considering a number of possible illnesses and then narrowing their focus to one.

Evaluation of the Biopsychosocial Factors

The biopsychosocial assessment is an all-encompassing method for gaining a better knowledge of the patient's situation. It takes into account the client's biological, psychological, and social variables, all of which contribute to their overall health.

1. Factors of a Biological Origin

The client's physical health, their genetics, and any medical disorders that the client may have that may have an affect on their mental and emotional well-being are all examples of biological factors.

In clinical practice, therapists take into account the ways in which the client's biological variables may affect both their mental health and the dynamics of their families.

2. Aspects of a Person's Psyche

Important Ideas The client's history of mental illness, personality, thought habits, and emotional well-being are all examples of psychological elements to consider.

Clinical application: In order to gain an understanding of the client's cognitive and emotional processes, therapists conduct psychological evaluations on their patients.

3. Affects from Society

The client's family, as well as their social support network, cultural background, and environmental influences, are all considered to be part of the client's social factors.

Application in the Clinical Setting: Therapists examine the client's social aspects to take into consideration how the client's family dynamics and cultural setting influence their well-being.

Developing Strategies for Treatment

Following the completion of the assessment, the next step for the therapist is to formulate the case and design the treatment. This involves putting together a complete case conceptualization and treatment plan by combining the findings of the evaluation.

1. The Construction of the Case

The creation of a full grasp of the client's issues, family dynamics, and the elements contributing to their worries is required for the development of a case.

Clinical Application: Therapists utilize case formulation as a guide to help them grasp the circumstances of the client, which ensures that they have a complete view of the client's issues.

2. The Planning of Treatment

The formulation of precise, measurable, achievable, relevant, and time-bound (SMART) goals, the selection of appropriate interventions, and the sketching of a plan for achieving therapeutic success are all essential components of treatment planning.

Clinical Application: Therapists work closely with their clients to develop treatment plans that take into account the clients' individual requirements and lay out a course of action for the client's future therapeutic growth.

Respect for Different Cultures

Domain II places a significant emphasis on cultural competence as an important component. It is essential to efficient practice to have a solid understanding of the role that cultural influences play in both treatment and evaluation.

1. Capacity for Intercultural Communication

Concepts Crucial to Understanding Understanding and respecting the distinct ideas, values, and experiences of customers who come from a variety of cultural backgrounds is an essential component of multicultural competency.

Clinical Application Therapists modify their evaluations so that they are culturally sensitive and take into account the specific requirements of their different clientele.

The Dynamics of the Family and Thinking in Systems

It is essential for MFTs to have a solid grasp of family dynamics as well as systemic thinking. In Domain II, you will be evaluated on your ability to perceive and understand family dynamics and roles within a systemic framework. This ability will be evaluated using the rubric provided.

1. The dynamics of the family

The relationships, roles, and patterns of communication that occur within a family system are all a part of what psychologists refer to as "family dynamics."

Clinical Application Therapists evaluate the client's family dynamics in order to gain an understanding of how those dynamics contribute to the client's presenting problems. They then utilize this information to inform both their evaluation and their treatment strategy.

2. Thinking in terms of systems

Important Ideas Realizing that changes in a single family member can have an effect on the entire family system is an essential part of practicing systems thinking.

Clinical application: Therapists collaborate with families to identify and address the impact of individual changes on the dynamic of the family, with the goal of fostering stronger relationships among family members.

Methods Used in Clinical Settings

Proficiency in using clinical techniques, therapies, and strategies is crucial in Domain II. This involves the ability to promote positive change within family structures, as well as to settle conflicts, enhance communication, and encourage positive change.

1. Methods Used in Clinical Settings

The concepts that are essential to understand are as follows: clinical approaches include a variety of interventions that try to promote positive change within family systems, facilitate communication, and resolve disputes.

Clinical Application: Therapists employ clinical procedures in order to treat particular problems and encourage healthy family dynamics.

Taking Into Account Ethical and Legal Implications

In the field of marriage and family therapy (MFT), adhering to ethical and legal standards is essential. Your understanding of the ethical principles and legal requirements that are specific to the profession will be evaluated in Domain II of the exam.

1. Fundamental Values and Beliefs

The concepts of informed consent, confidentiality, and professional boundaries are some examples of the key concepts that are included in ethical principles.

Clinical Application: Therapists ensure that the rights of their clients are respected and that ethical norms are followed by adhering to ethical principles in their practices.

2. Considerations from a Legal Standpoint

The laws and regulations that govern the practice of MFT in California need to be comprehended in order to properly address the legal aspects of the situation.

Clinical Application: Therapists ensure that they are in conformity with legal standards by adhering to the rules and regulations that regulate their practice.

3. Conducting Studies and Analyses

In order to pass Domain II, you need to demonstrate that you have an awareness of research methodology and evaluation processes. Utilizing research in order to improve and inform clinical practice is part of this process.

1. Techniques for Conducting Research

Principal Ideas: The term "research methodologies" refers to a wide range of approaches to the process of conducting research, including both qualitative and quantitative procedures.

Clinical application refers to the process by which therapists can use the findings of research to inform their practice and keep themselves apprised of the most recent advancements in their area.

2. The Processes of Evaluation

The evaluation process involves determining how beneficial various treatment methods are and acting on that information based on your findings.

Clinical Application: Therapists make use of evaluation techniques in order to gauge the development that their clients are making and to make required alterations to their treatment programs.

Tips for Achieving Success in Domain II of the Clinical Assessment, Diagnosis, and Treatment Planning Exams

Now that you have a thorough comprehension of Domain II, the following are some pointers that will help you do exceptionally well in this domain:

1. Examine the Various Methods of Evaluation

Spend some time familiarizing yourself with a variety of evaluation techniques, such as personal interviews, standardized tests, family assessment tools, and genograms. To improve your skills, put these strategies into practice by acting out hypothetical events.

2. Develop Robust Capabilities in the Art of Diagnosis

Learn the DSM criteria, as well as the procedure of differential diagnosis, and get familiar with both. Perform diagnoses on fictitious patients depending on the symptoms they are exhibiting and the results of your assessments of them.

3. Evaluation of the Biopsychosocial Factors

Acquire an understanding of the various aspects that comprise a biopsychosocial examination. Conducting assessments that take into account biological, psychological, and social variables should become second nature.

4. Formulation of the Case and Planning of the Treatment

Develop your skills in case analysis and treatment planning by working with made-up examples of fictional patients. The development of tailored and all-encompassing treatment regimens should be the primary focus.

5. Consideration of Other Cultures

Culture sensitivity should be given careful consideration. You should become familiar with the cultural elements that can influence evaluation and treatment planning, and you should practice changing your approach to meet the particular requirements of clients who come from a variety of backgrounds.

6. Have an understanding of the dynamics of the family and of systems thinking

Recognize the significance of family dynamics and thinking about the system as a whole when doing the assessment and planning the treatment. Think about how the actions of one family member might have repercussions for the entire family unit.

7. Make Use of Different Clinical Techniques

It is important to put into practice therapeutic strategies and interventions that will help to improve communication, bring about the resolution of conflicts, and encourage positive transformation within family systems. Playing roles and participating in exercises based on simulated situations might be beneficial.

8. Considerations Regarding Ethical and Legal Implications

Be sure that you have a solid comprehension of the ethical concepts and legal standards that are applicable to your line of work. Maintain a level of awareness of the most recent changes to the applicable rules and regulations.

9. Research and Critical Analysis

Get yourself acquainted with the various research methodologies and analysis procedures. Prepare yourself to incorporate the findings of research into your therapeutic work in order to improve it.

10. Seek Out Supervision and Guidance from Others

You could want to look into getting supervision or guidance from more experienced MFTs. They are able to provide direction, insights into practical situations, and invaluable counsel regarding the assessment, diagnostic, and treatment planning processes.

11. Methods of Making Ethical Decisions in Practice

Participate in activities that focus on ethical decision-making to improve your ability to solve ethical problems that may crop up throughout the assessment and treatment planning stages of a project.

12. Ensure That You Keep Up with the Latest Research

Maintain an up-to-date knowledge of the most recent advancements in the methods of evaluation and treatment planning. Because of the rapid pace of change in the field of therapy, it is critical that you keep abreast of recent developments.

Domain III, or the Psychotherapeutic and Counseling Relationship, is discussed in Chapter 8.

The psychotherapeutic and counseling relationship is the primary focal point of Domain III of the Marriage and Family Therapy (MFT) Exam in the state of California. Due to the fact that the therapeutic connection is the foundation of successful therapy, this area is of the utmost importance when it comes to the practice of marital and family therapy. The purpose of this chapter is to provide you with a full grasp of the therapeutic relationship, including important concepts, strategies, and ethical considerations by delving into the specifics of Domain III as we proceed through this chapter.

Comprehending the Role of the Therapist in the Process

Within the realm of marriage and family therapy, the therapeutic relationship serves as the bedrock upon which successful treatment is built. It includes the interactions, dynamics, and rapport that are developed between the therapist and the client or clients in the course of therapy. In the third domain, your expertise and knowledge will be evaluated on the establishment, maintenance, and management of the therapeutic relationship.

1. The Alliance for Therapeutic

Concepts Crucial to Understanding The term "therapeutic alliance" refers to the nature of the relationship that exists between the client and the therapist. It involves things like trust, rapport, and working together.

Application in the Clinic Therapists seek to establish a strong therapeutic alliance with their clients by cultivating trust and making certain that their patients feel heard and valued.

2. Limits and confines

In the context of the therapeutic interaction, it is essential to establish and uphold appropriate boundaries at all times. Within the setting of therapy, limits and expectations are delineated through the use of boundaries.

Clinical Application Therapists set defined limits in order to retain their professionalism, safeguard their clients' health, and ensure that the therapeutic environment is conducive to healing.

3. Having a Cultural Awareness

Concepts Essential to Understanding Understanding and respecting the distinctive cultural ideas, attitudes, and experiences of clients who come from a variety of backgrounds is the cornerstone of cultural competency in the therapeutic partnership.

The clinical application of this concept is that therapists modify their methods so that they are culturally sensitive, so ensuring that clients from a variety of backgrounds feel understood and valued.

4. Focus on the Needs of the Customers

Conceptually, the client is placed at the center of the therapeutic process using the client-centered approach, which gives the client the opportunity to actively participate in their own therapy.

In clinical practice, it is important for therapists to involve their clients in the planning of their treatment, to respect their autonomy, and to encourage patients to discuss their hopes and fears.

5. Compassion

Empathy is defined as the capacity to comprehend and share the sentiments of another person, specifically the client. It is absolutely necessary for the development of a solid therapeutic connection.

The clinical application of empathy is when therapists engage with their patients on an emotional level in order to transmit understanding and support to their patients.

6. Engaging in attentive listening

Important Ideas: Active listening entails spending one's whole attention on what the customer is saying in order to completely comprehend it and provide a suitable response to it. It encourages honest communication as well as trust.

Application in the Clinical Setting: Therapists should engage in active listening in order to cultivate an atmosphere in which patients feel heard and respected.

7. Communicating Without Speaking

Nonverbal communication can be broken down into its component parts, which are gestures, body language, facial expressions, and tone of voice. In the context of the therapeutic relationship, it is an important factor in the expression of feelings and the development of understanding.

In clinical practice, it is important for therapists to be aware of their own nonverbal cues as well as those of their clients in order to facilitate communication that is both accurate and consistent.

8. Respect and Acknowledgement of Others

The therapeutic relationship is built on a foundation of mutual respect and acceptance between the parties involved. The client must feel as though their therapist is accepting of them and is not passing judgment on them.

The clinical application of this principle is that therapists should respect the client's autonomy, decisions, and experiences in order to foster an environment in which patients are comfortable being open and honest.

Considerations of an Ethical Nature

The therapeutic relationship must adhere to a set of ethical norms and guidelines in order to safeguard the client's rights and ensure their wellbeing. In Domain III, you will be evaluated on both your understanding of ethical principles as well as your ability to navigate ethical dilemmas that arise within the context of the therapeutic interaction.

1. Free and Voluntary Consent

The concept of giving one's consent after being fully informed is an important one in ethics. The client is required to give their consent before participating in the treatment process, as well as to be informed about the procedure itself, their rights, and the therapist's approach.

Before beginning therapy with a client, therapists should make sure that the client has a thorough understanding of the process of treatment, as well as any associated risks, benefits, and confidentiality policies.

2. Maintaining strict secrecy

Important Ideas: The client's right to privacy can be safeguarded by adhering to the confidentiality principle. With a few legal and ethical exemptions, therapists are required to maintain client confidentiality about any and all material shared during sessions.

Clinical application: therapists maintain strong confidentiality with their clients, only disclosing information about a client when required to do so by law or when the client gives their written approval.

3. Relationships With Two People

Conceptually, a dual relationship exists between a therapist and a client when the therapist fulfills more than one role in the client's life, such as being a family friend, a coworker, or an employer. The avoidance of dual partnerships is emphasized in ethical rules.

The clinical application of this principle requires that therapists uphold professional boundaries and steer clear of dual relationships that could undermine the effectiveness of their work.

4. Taking Control of the Countertransference

The term "countertransference" refers to the emotional reactions and responses of the therapist to the client. In order to preserve one's objectivity, it is essential to be aware of and effectively manage countertransference.

In clinical practice, it is important for therapists to be aware of their own countertransference reactions and to seek supervision or assistance whenever necessary in order to prevent these reactions from having a negative impact on the therapeutic relationship.

5. The Finishing of the Treatment

Important Ideas: When therapy is terminated, the therapeutic connection must be ended in a way that is both intentional and ethical. It is an important procedure that has to be carefully considered and talked about.

Clinical Application: Therapists collaborate with clients to plan and carry out the process of terminating therapy, ensuring that it is done so in an ethical manner and in a manner that serves the client's best interests.

6. Reporting cases of abuse against children and the elderly

The following are some important concepts to keep in mind: Therapists have a moral as well as a legal obligation to report any suspected cases of child or elder abuse to the proper authorities.

The clinical application of this is that therapists need to be informed of the laws and rules regulating the reporting of abuse against children and the elderly, and they need to fulfill their duty to safeguard clients who are vulnerable.

Methods Used in Clinical Settings

In Domain III, your understanding of clinical procedures for constructing and sustaining a therapeutic relationship will be evaluated. This domain's focus is on assessment of clinical skills. These methods are crucial for establishing a therapeutic setting that is both secure and encouraging to patients.

1. Methods of Reflection and Introspection

In order to improve a person's level of self-awareness, reflective procedures entail the client's thoughts, feelings, and experiences being reflected back to them.

Application in the Clinical Setting: Therapists make use of reflective techniques to assist patients in exploring their feelings and gaining a greater understanding of their concerns.

2. Capabilities in Communicating

The ability to actively listen, empathize, and show understanding and support are essential components of effective communication abilities.

In clinical practice, therapists make use of their excellent communication skills to develop rapport with their clients and encourage candid and open discussion.

3. Responding to Emergencies

When clients are in urgent danger or distress, approaches for crisis intervention are employed to help them through the situation. The provision of instant support and help is the primary focus of these methods.

In clinical practice, this means that therapists are ready to implement crisis intervention strategies whenever they are required to do so in order to protect the client's safety and wellbeing.

4. Counseling Strategies for Individuals, Families, and Couples

Concepts Essential To Understanding These therapeutic strategies for families and couples are aimed to address relational challenges, improve healthy communication, and facilitate the settlement of conflicts.

In clinical practice, therapists make use of specialized approaches in order to address the dynamics and issues of couples and families in order to facilitate positive transformation.

Supervision, as well as care for oneself

In order to safeguard their health and continue practicing effectively, therapists frequently seek out supervision and participate in activities designed to promote self-care. In Domain III, your comprehension of the significance of being supervised as well as taking care of oneself will be evaluated.

1. Supervision in Clinical Settings

The overarching goal of clinical supervision is to improve clinical competence while also addressing ethical and clinical conundrums. This is accomplished by seeking advice and assistance from more seasoned supervisors.

Clinical application: It is possible for therapists to participate in clinical supervision in order to get feedback, direction, and assistance in the process of resolving difficult situations and ethical difficulties.

2. Methods of Caring for Oneself

Important Ideas: In order to keep one's mental and physical health in good shape, it is necessary for a therapist to engage in self-care practices. They contribute to the protection against burnout and exhaustion caused by compassion.

In clinical practice, it is important for therapists to make self-care a priority by engaging in activities such as exercising, practicing mindfulness, and going to their own therapy sessions. This helps them maintain their emotional resilience and competence.

Tips for Achieving Success in Domain III: The Therapeutic Relationship

Consider the following advice for establishing and maintaining a healthy therapeutic connection so that you can excel in Domain III:

1. Take a look at the Therapeutic Alliance.

Realize how important it is to construct a solid partnership for therapeutic purposes. Putting into practice strategies for establishing rapport, trust, and collaboration with customers is essential.

2. Define your limits and stick to them.

Figure out how to set and maintain appropriate boundaries within the context of the therapeutic partnership. Drive home the point that professionalism and precaution are of the utmost importance.

3. Having a Cultural Awareness

Maintaining cultural competency should be a top priority, and the best way to achieve this is to become familiar with the cultural aspects that can impact the therapeutic interaction. Modify your strategy so that it can cater to the specific requirements of a wide variety of customers.

4. Focus on the Needs of the Customers

Embrace a client-centered approach that places a premium on the client's autonomy and gives them the tools necessary to take an active part in their own therapy.

5. Develop your capacity for empathy and attentive listening.

To cultivate a setting in which customers are given the impression that they are heard and respected, work on improving your ability to empathize with customers and engage in practices of active listening.

6. Respect and Acknowledgement of Others

Show clients respect and acceptance, and strive to create an environment that is accepting, non-judgmental, and supportive so that clients can feel free to express themselves openly.

7. Gain an Awareness of the Ethical Considerations

Acquaint yourself with the ethical standards that should guide your work, such as informed permission, confidentiality, and the proper handling of dual relationships. Prepare yourself to deal with difficult ethical situations that may arise in the course of the therapeutic interaction.

8. Make Use of Different Clinical Techniques

In order to cultivate a therapeutic relationship that is both helpful and efficient, it is important to put clinical procedures, such as reflective techniques, robust communication skills, and crisis intervention tactics, into practice.

9. Seek Supervision, and Make Caring for Yourself a Top Priority

Recognize the value of clinical supervision in helping you improve your skills and address both clinical and ethical issues. In addition, make the maintenance of your emotional toughness and overall well-being a top priority by engaging in self-care routines.

10. Ensure Continued Sensitivity to Culture

Keep learning about cultural competency, and make sure you're up to date on the cultural issues that could effect your therapy partnership. Adjust your strategy so that it takes into account the specific requirements of each individual customer.

The fourth domain, "Professional Ethics, Law, Regulation, and Policies," is covered in Chapter 9.

The professional ethics, laws, regulations, and policies of the profession are the primary emphasis of the Domain IV of the California Marriage and Family Therapy (MFT) Exam. This area of responsibility is absolutely essential for ensuring that marriage and family therapists (MFTs) conduct their practices in an ethical manner and in accordance with the legal norms that regulate their profession. The purpose of this chapter is to provide you with a full grasp of the professional ethics, legal issues, and rules that guide the practice of marriage and family therapy by delving into the specifics of Domain IV.

Ethics in the Professions

Marriage and family therapists are held to a set of moral standards and norms known as "professional ethics," which governs their behavior and how they interact with their clients. In Domain IV, you will be evaluated on both your knowledge of professional ethics and your capacity to put that knowledge into practice in a variety of scenarios.

1. A moral and ethical code

Key Ideas: The Code of Ethics is a set of ethical rules produced by professional organizations, such as the American Association for Marriage and Family Therapy (AAMFT), that describes the ethical principles and standards for marriage and family therapists (MFTs).

Clinical Application Therapists are required to comply with the Code of Ethics in their work, which ensures that their behavior is in line with the ethical standards that have been established.

2. Consent After Being Informed

Informed consent is a core ethical notion that requires therapists to seek the client's voluntary and informed permission to participate in treatment. This agreement must be obtained before the client can be treated.

The clinical application of this principle requires therapists to gain informed permission from their clients by outlining the nature and method of therapy, as well as its risks and benefits, policies regarding confidentiality, and the client's rights.

3. Maintaining strict secrecy

Important Ideas: The ethical principle of confidentiality protects both the client's private and the client's right to have their privacy respected. It is an essential component of both ethical behavior and trustworthiness in business.

Clinical Application Therapists are obligated to maintain tight confidentiality at all times, preserving both the personal and therapeutic information of their clients. Exceptions to this rule include situations in which they are required to divulge the information by law or when they have the client's consent.

4. Multiple Romantic Partnerships

Conceptually, a dual relationship exists between a therapist and a client when the therapist fulfills more than one role in the client's life, such as being a family friend, a coworker, or an employer. The need of avoiding parallel relationships that could put the therapeutic one at risk is emphasized by the ethical rules.

The clinical application of this principle requires that therapists keep their professional boundaries intact and steer clear of dual relationships that might compromise either their impartiality or the therapeutic relationship.

5. Capability and Participation in Ongoing Education

Concepts Essential to Understanding Competence is an ethical requirement that requires therapists to deliver treatments only within their domains of competence and to engage in ongoing professional development by participating in continuing education.

Clinical Application: In order to offer quality care, therapists are required to consistently evaluate and improve their level of competence, as well as seek out more training and education when appropriate.

6. Accountability in the Professional World

Concepts Crucial: To uphold one's ethical commitments, fulfill one's legal responsibilities, and fulfill one's professional obligations in order to protect the interests of one's clients is the essence of professional responsibility.

Application in the Clinic Therapists have the responsibility of respecting ethical standards and legislation while also providing their clients with care that is both competent and ethical.

7. Making Decisions in an Ethical Manner

Concepts Crucial: The process of detecting ethical challenges, considering various courses of action, and making ethical decisions that emphasize the well-being of the client are all aspects of the decision-making process that go into ethical decision-making.

Application in the Clinic Therapists need to be skilled in ethical decision-making in order to successfully traverse the difficult situations and conundrums that may come up during treatment.

Taking into account the law

Domain IV places a significant emphasis on the importance of legal matters. Marriage and family therapists have a responsibility to their clients to conform to the laws and regulations that govern their field of activity in order to safeguard their clients' legal and physical interests.

1. Obtaining the Required Permits and Certifications

In order to legally work as a marriage and family therapist (MFT), one must first obtain a license and then certification. It is necessary for therapists to first earn the right credentials and then keep those credentials current throughout their careers.

Clinical Application: In order to legally perform their profession, therapists need to guarantee that they hold the appropriate licenses and certifications. This includes fulfilling all of the requirements for renewal as well as ongoing education.

2. The Reporting of Abuse of Children and the Elderly

Important Ideas: Counselors have a moral and ethical responsibility to notify the proper authorities whenever they feel that a client is abusing a youngster or an elderly person. Protecting those who are weak or defenseless requires us to do this important work.

Clinical Application: Therapists have a responsibility to disclose any suspected instances of child or elder abuse, and they must be knowledgeable of the laws and regulations that govern the reporting of such abuse.

3. Maintaining privacy in accordance with HIPAA

Important Ideas: Laws pertaining to confidentiality, such as the Health Insurance Portability and Accountability Act (HIPAA), are responsible for establishing the legal requirements that must be followed in order to protect the privacy of client information.

Clinical Relevance Therapists are required to comply with confidentiality laws and the standards of HIPAA, which ensures that client information is properly managed and preserved.

4. The Caution of Tarasoff

Important Ideas: The Tarasoff warning refers to a legal obligation for therapists to warn potential victims when a client poses a danger of harm to others. In other words, when a client poses a risk of harm to others, therapists have a duty to do so.

Application in the Clinical Setting: Therapists need to be aware that it is their responsibility to intervene and protect possible victims in cases where a client poses a risk of damage to others.

5. Counseling Required by the Court

Concepts Crucial: If a client is subject to court-ordered therapy, the therapist may be required to offer services to the client in accordance with the directives of the court or other legal authority.

When offering therapy to clients who are involved in legal procedures, therapists are required to adhere to legal regulations and court orders in order to maintain their clinical license.

6. The Breadth of Our Work

The legal constraints of what therapists can and cannot do within the context of their profession are outlined in the "scope of practice," which is a key concept.

Clinical Application Therapists have a responsibility to conduct their work within the legal parameters of their profession, avoiding any acts or interventions that go beyond the extent of their authorized scope of practice.

7. Obstacles of a Moral and Legal Nature

In the course of their work, therapists may find themselves confronted with difficult ethical and legal issues, such as conundrums involving compulsory reporting, dual partnerships, or confidentiality concerns.

Clinical Application: Therapists need to have the knowledge and abilities necessary to address and negotiate these obstacles while also preserving ethical standards and complying with legal regulations.

Policy and Regulatory Frameworks

As part of the evaluation for Domain IV, you will also be tested on how well you comprehend the more general regulations and policies that direct the marriage and family therapy profession.

1. Regulations at the State and Federal Level

Concepts crucial to this understanding: the legal basis for the practice of MFTs is provided by state and federal regulations. These regulations are different in each state.

The clinical application of this principle requires therapists to be aware of the specific state and federal regulations that are pertinent to their line of work and to conduct themselves in accordance with those restrictions.

2. Boards of Examiners for Professional Practices and Other Professional Organizations

Standards and guidelines for MFTs are established by licensing boards and professional organizations like the Board of Behavioral Sciences and the American Association of Marriage and Family Therapists (AAMFT).

Clinical application: It is the responsibility of therapists to remain knowledgeable about the regulations and standards that are established by licensing boards and professional organizations, and to adhere to these policies and standards in their work.

3. Insurance against Medical Errors

Key Ideas: misconduct insurance is a subtype of professional liability insurance that shields therapists from the financial and professional consequences of being sued for negligence or misconduct.

In clinical settings, it is recommended that therapists investigate the possibility of purchasing malpractice insurance as a means of defending oneself against potential legal actions stemming from their professional activities.

4. Maintaining Records and Providing Documentation

Important Ideas: For both ethical and legal reasons, it is necessary to maintain and document records in a manner that is both accurate and exhaustive. They offer a transparent record of the treatment process and are frequently mandated by legal authorities.

The clinical application of this is that therapists are required to keep records of client interactions and interventions that are both detailed and secure in order to comply with legal and ethical obligations.

5. Consultation and Oversight of Operations

The ability of therapists to engage in ethical and professional practices that are supported by regular supervision and consultation is crucial to their professional development. When confronted with difficult cases or ethical conundrums, therapists frequently seek supervision and guidance from colleagues.

Clinical Application: Therapists may choose to participate in supervision and consultation in order to improve their level of expertise and their ability to make ethical decisions.

Guidelines for Achieving Success in Domain IV: Professional Ethics, Law, Regulation, and Policies

Consider the following advice for gaining a grasp of and using professional ethics, legal issues, and rules so that you can excel in Domain IV:

1. Familiarize yourself with the Code of Ethics.

Get yourself acquainted with the Code of Ethics that applies to your profession, such as the AAMFT Code of Ethics, for example. Acquire a solid understanding of the moral guidelines and professional norms that direct your work.

2. Ensure That You Are Always Up-to-Date On All Legal Requirements

Maintain a level of familiarity with the particular legal standards and laws that are applicable in your state. The direction and up-to-date information on legal standards might be provided by licensing boards and professional organizations.

3. Participate in Educational Refresher Courses

Participate in ongoing educational opportunities to maintain your relevance in the face of rapid changes in the industry's legal and ethical landscapes. The value of attending seminars and workshops on morality, jurisprudence, and administrative rules cannot be overstated.

4. Be sure to keep documentation and records.

Establish rigorous record-keeping methods to guarantee that your documentation is in accordance with all applicable legal and ethical requirements. This involves keeping records of informed consent, progress notes, and any required reporting that may be required.

5. Seek Out Supervision and Advice from Others

When confronted with difficult issues or ethical conundrums, don't be afraid to seek supervision and guidance from a more experienced professional. Supervisors who have prior experience are in the best position to provide direction and assistance in overcoming these obstacles.

6. Be mindful of your obligations to the profession.

Uphold your professional responsibilities by adhering to the ethical standards set for your profession and conducting your work within the bounds of its purview. Maintain a commitment to the standards of professional ethics while giving the health and happiness of your customers top priority.

7. Acquire an Awareness of, and Compliance with, Existing Confidentiality Laws

In order to maintain the confidentiality of your customers' information and safeguard their safety, you should make sure that you have a thorough understanding of applicable confidentiality regulations, such as HIPAA, and that you comply with these laws.

8. Put Yourself in a Position to Make Ethical Decisions

Decision-making that is ethical should be practiced, and practitioners should be ready to handle ethical conundrums in their work. Think about what might happen in hypothetical situations and make moral decisions that put the satisfaction of your customers first.

9. Give Some Thought to Professional Liability Insurance

If you want to protect yourself from potential legal claims that are associated with your profession, you should think about purchasing malpractice insurance. Discuss your requirements with the companies that provide insurance.

10. Examine the relevant local, state, and federal regulations

Maintain a level of familiarity with the myriad of state and federal regulations that are particular to your area of practice. For this purpose, it may be necessary to research the regulations and policies that have been established by the licensing board in your state and other professional organizations.

Exam-Day Strategies is the topic of Chapter 10.

The California Marriage and Family Therapy (MFT) Exam is the capstone of the process that leads to obtaining a license to practice marriage and family therapy in the state of California (LMFT). Even though your preparation up to this point has been essential, in order to do well on the actual test, you will also need to use certain successful methods. In this chapter, we will talk about methods that you can use on the day of the exam to help you approach the MFT Exam with confidence, manage test anxiety, and maximize your performance.

Before the Day of the Exam

The studying is not the end of your preparation for the MFT Exam; there are numerous important measures to do in the days preceding up to the exam, including the following:

Spend the last few days before the test going over your study materials and making sure everything is correct. Spend most of your time concentrating on the essential ideas, notes, flashcards, and practice questions. Reinforce what you already know rather than trying to learn new stuff; this will save you time.

To simulate the settings of the exam, you should create an atmosphere that is calm, free of distractions, and similar to the actual test conditions. It is recommended that you become accustomed to the time constraint by practicing with timed, full-length practice tests.

In the interest of organization, check to see that you possess all of the required forms of identity and documentation. Verify that the examination will take place at the specified location and time, and compile a list of everything else that must be brought with you.

approaches for Relaxation and Breathing Exercises Deep breathing exercises, meditation, and yoga are all examples of stress management approaches. Getting enough sleep and maintaining a healthy diet are two of the most important factors in lowering stress levels.

Making Travel Arrangements: Make travel arrangements to get to the testing location. Check that you are familiar with the place, and make sure that you have a strategy for getting there on time. Consider the likelihood of delays caused by traffic.

The Morning of the Exam

It is critical to have a well-prepared strategy as well as a positive mental attitude on the morning of the test:

Arrive Early: You need to get to the testing location as early as possible. Give yourself some buffer time in case something comes up that you weren't expecting. If you get to the test early, it will be easier for you to start it in a calm state of mind.

Proper Nourishment Eat a well-rounded breakfast and be sure to drink enough of water. Caffeine consumption in excess can cause jitteriness and anxiety, so try to limit how much you take in. Choose a meal that offers a variety of nutrients, such as protein, complex carbohydrates, and a few servings of healthy fats.

One more review tip: while you eat breakfast, skim over your important notes or review flashcards briefly. Do not make an effort to learn anything new; the purpose of this exercise is only to jog your memory.

Affirmations Positive: If you want to feel more confident, try using affirmations that focus on the positive. Bring to your mind the amount of effort that you have put into getting ready for this.

Exercises in Mindfulness and Relaxation In order to calm your anxieties, you can do exercises in mindfulness or relaxation techniques. Exercising your diaphragm through deep breathing might be especially helpful.

When it comes to the Exam

After entering the testing room, you should direct your attention to effective test-taking tactics in order to make the most of your performance:

Take Your Time to Read the Instructions and Questions Take your time to read the questions and instructions carefully. It's possible to give the wrong answer if you misinterpret the question.

It is recommended that you begin by responding to the questions you feel the most comfortable answering. Taking this strategy enables you to increase your confidence and secure simple points.

Time Management: Always be aware of what time it is. The MFT Exam is timed, and you should make it a goal to devote a predetermined amount of your total allotted time to each question. Mark the question for subsequent review if you have any doubts about how to respond to it.

The process of elimination is a method that can be utilized in order to reduce the number of possible answers. If you want to maximize your odds of picking the right answer, you should start by eliminating the choices that you know for a fact are wrong.

Marking Questions for study If there is a question that you do not fully understand, you should mark it for further study before continuing. Don't become stuck on a single solution for an excessive amount of time. You are free to return to it at a later time if time permits.

Keeping Calm: Maintain your composure and your concentration. When confronted with a difficult question, it's important to take a moment to gather your composure and think back on the material you studied. Anxiety can make it difficult to think clearly.

Pacing: Ensure that you keep a steady pace for the entirety of the test. Being too sluggish can prevent you from answering all of the questions, while rushing can make you more likely to make thoughtless mistakes.

After you have finished the first pass through the questions, you should revisit the ones that were marked as incorrect and give them another look. Please go back and look over these questions as well as your answers. If you are not certain that your response is incorrect, you should refrain from changing it.

Remember that you can obtain partial credit for multiple-choice questions, as this type of question gives you the opportunity to do so. Even if you don't know the answer for sure, you should make the best approximation you can.

Pauses for the Mind If the test is very long, you might want to think about taking a few brief mental rests. To bring your thoughts back into focus, stand up, do some stretching, and take some deep breaths.

The Handling of Anxiety

Anxiety before exams is rather frequent, but there are effective ways to manage it, including the following:

Exercises in Deep Breathing Taking part in exercises that focus on deep breathing will help calm your nervous system. First, take a slow breath in via your nose, then hold your breath for a few seconds, and finally, exhale through your mouth.

Visualization: Picture yourself succeeding in what you're trying to accomplish. Imagine that you are answering questions with self-assurance and that you have successfully completed the test.

Replace negative ideas with positive statements to yourself using positive self-talk. Bring to remember the amount of time you spent preparing and how well you already know the content.

To alleviate both mental and physical stress, practitioners of progressive muscle relaxation instruct patients to tense and then relax certain groups of muscles.

Meditation on Mindfulness: Practice mindfulness meditation to help you remain present in the moment and stop your mind from racing with worrisome thoughts; it will help you stay in the here and now.

strategies for Grounding: Using strategies for grounding, such as counting to ten or concentrating on an object in the room, can assist in bringing you back to the here and now and reducing the amount of anxiety you feel.

After Completing the Exam

After the test is done, it is very important to evaluate how well you did and think about the steps that you should take next:

Avoid Having Discussions About the Exam Right After It You should make every effort to avoid having discussions about the exam with other people right after it. Conversations after an exam have the potential to mislead people and generate undue concern.

Take some time for yourself to relax and unwind, and then give yourself a reward for your hard work. To relieve stress, you should take part in activities that you enjoy.

Plan for Results: While you're waiting for your results, make a plan for what you'll do with your time. Whether it involves continuing to study or taking a break that's long overdue, having a plan might help ease the tension that comes after an exam.

Gain Knowledge Through Experience: Consider what you learned from your test. Think about the aspects of your preparation and test-taking tactics that worked well and those that could use some tweaking.

Get ready for the next steps: if you don't pass the test, don't let it get you down. There are a great number of people that fail their initial effort. Make use of the experience to help you determine areas in which you can develop, and keep up your efforts.

Maintain Your Perspective: It is important to keep in mind that passing the exam is just one step on the path to becoming a licensed marriage and family therapist (LMFT). Your commitment, continued progress, and enthusiasm for the industry are of equal significance.

Attempting the Test Once More

In the sad event that you do not pass the exam, it is absolutely necessary to keep a positive attitude and formulate a strategy for retaking it:

Conduct an analysis of your results to determine which aspects of your performance went well and which ones could use some work. Your performance will be broken down for you in the report on the examination.

Make Changes to Your Study Method: Make changes to your study method based on the results of your performance analysis. Concentrate more on the aspects in which you had difficulty.

In order to improve the quality of your preparation, you should investigate the possibility of receiving assistance from instructors, study groups, or other sources.

Manage Your Test Anxiety If you feel that anxiety is affecting your performance, you should spend more time practicing strategies to relax and manage stress.

You should try to repeat the test by signing up for it again and making the most of the knowledge you gained from the first time you took it.

Remember your enthusiasm for the profession, as well as your dedication to working toward being a licensed mental health counselor. The path to success is frequently paved with perseverance.

After You've Passed the Test: The Next Steps Towards Getting Your License

On your successful completion of the Marriage and Family Therapy (MFT) Exam in the state of California, congrats! On your path to obtaining a license as a Marriage and Family Therapist (LMFT) in the state of California, you have just passed a critical milestone. Congratulations! In this chapter, we will discuss what to anticipate after the exam, the measures you need to follow to get closer to obtaining your license, and the professional prospects that are waiting for you when you pass the exam.

Obtaining the Results of Your Examination

Following the completion of the MFT Exam, you will anxiously wait for the results. Exam results are normally made available within a few weeks after being requested from the California Board of Behavioral Sciences (BBS), the governing body that is responsible for the licensing procedure. You will be informed of your performance on the test, including whether or not you passed it. Keep in mind that it is not unusual for folks to need more than one go at the test in order to achieve the desired result. Do not feel disheartened if you did not pass the test this time. Make use of the experience to help you determine which aspects of your studying and test-taking skills could use some work.

Getting Ready to Receive One's License

If you were successful on the MFT Exam, then you are one step closer to receiving your license. To become a licensed marriage and family therapist in the state of California, you will need to finish a few additional stages first. These steps include the following:

Accumulating Supervised Experience In order to be eligible to submit an application for licensing, you are required to complete a predetermined amount of hours of supervised clinical experience. The BBS requires that you work a minimum of 3,000 hours spread out over a period of at least two years. During this time period, you are going to need to locate a qualified supervisor who can watch over your work.

Receiving Supervision: While participating in your supervised experience, your supervisor will provide you with direction, feedback, and assistance on a regular basis. They will assist you in enhancing your clinical abilities, navigating ethical conundrums, and fulfilling the criteria of the BBS.

Application for licensing: Once you have amassed the necessary number of hours of supervised experience, you are eligible to submit an application for licensing with the BBS. The submission of transcripts, evidence that the applicant has been supervised, and any other pertinent documentation is normally required throughout the application process. Your application will be evaluated by the BBS, and your eligibility for a license will be confirmed.

In addition to the MFT Exam, you will need to pass the California Law and Ethics Exam for LMFTs in order to become licensed as a marriage and family therapist in the state of California. Your knowledge of the legal and ethical principles that govern your profession will be evaluated based on your performance on this exam.

Background Check In order to become licensed by the BBS, applicants are need to pass a background check first. Make sure that your history does not include any problems that might prevent you from obtaining a license if you apply for one.

Completing Additional Requirements It's possible that, given your specific circumstances, you'll need to complete some additional requirements. Taking care of any violations of the law or of ethical standards, submitting to additional supervision, or attending particular classes could all fall under this category.

Acquiring Professional Liability Insurance Being a practicing therapist requires you to obtain professional liability insurance in order to safeguard both yourself and your clients. Before you can start your clinical practice, you are going to need to make sure you have this insurance.

Beginning Your Clinical Practice Once you have been awarded your LMFT license, you are prepared to start your professional journey and can begin your clinical practice. You have the opportunity to work in an established therapy facility, begin your own private practice, or investigate the many other career paths available in the profession.

Opportunities for Professional Careers for LMFTs

When you earn your certification as a marriage and family therapist, a wide variety of professional doors will open for you. These may include the following:

Private Practice: Many licensed marriage and family therapists (LMFTs) opt to start their own private therapy clinics. This provides the potential for autonomy, flexibility, and the chance to work with clients on a wide range of difficulties, ranging from problems in their relationships to concerns about their mental health.

Participating in a group therapy practice gives you the opportunity to network with other people who work in the mental health field, exchange information and materials, and do your job in an encouraging atmosphere.

Community Mental Health Centers: These facilities offer essential assistance to disadvantaged families and people in the local community. You can obtain useful experience in community-based settings while working with a variety of client demographics if you have your LMFT.

Hospitals and other medical facilities: LMFTs are frequently employed by hospitals to assist patients and the relatives of those patients. This may involve assisting families in adjusting to medical diagnosis or giving counseling services at times of medical emergency.

LMFTs are able to work in educational settings such as schools, colleges, and universities, where they provide support to students, faculty, and staff members who are dealing with a variety of personal and academic issues.

drug misuse Treatment Centers: LMFTs can specialize in aiding individuals and families affected by drug misuse and addiction. They play an important role in the recovery process by providing assistance to those affected on both an individual and family level.

Crisis and Trauma therapy Many licensed marriage and family therapists (LMFTs) have specialized training in the field of crisis and trauma therapy. In this capacity, they offer support to individuals and families who are coping with traumatic experiences, such as the aftermath of a natural catastrophe or an act of violence.

Services for Military Members and Veterans: LMFTs are able to work with service members, veterans, and the families of both groups to address the special issues that are associated with military service and deployments.

Consultation and Supervision: Seasoned LMFTs may decide to pursue careers as supervisors or consultants, so contributing to the education of future generations of therapists and offering their experience to other organizations.

Education and Training for Working Professionals (Continuing Education and Training)

Becoming a licensed marriage and family therapist is not the conclusion of your educational journey; rather, it is just the beginning. You will be required to participate in ongoing professional development and continuing education in order to keep your license active and keep up with the latest developments in the area. This may entail the following:

CEUs, which stands for continuing education units, are mandated by the majority of jurisdictions, including California, for licensed therapists to regularly complete a certain number of CEUs. These units may consist of workshops, seminars, or courses that bring you up to speed on the most recent advancements in your field of study.

If you are a supervisor of intern therapists, you may be required to take part in ongoing supervision in order to assist the intern therapists' continued growth and development.

Specializations: If you are interested in a certain field, you should think about getting specialized training or certifications in that field. This can help you stand out from the competition and expand the job alternatives available to you.

Joining a professional organization, such as the American Association for Marriage and Family Therapy (AAMFT), can give you access to a variety of tools, as well as opportunities to make connections with other people and the most recent findings in the field.

Participating in Industry Conferences and Workshops Attending industry conferences and workshops is a great way to increase your expertise, connect with colleagues in your field, and learn about emerging trends.

Publications and Research: If you want to build your professional profile and make a contribution to the expansion of your field, you should consider publishing research or writing articles in your area of expertise.

Ethical Conduct and the Maintenance of One's Health

It is essential to a successful career as an LMFT to uphold ethical standards in one's practice and place a high priority on one's own self-care.

Ethical principles It is imperative that you continue to conduct yourself in accordance with the ethical principles established for your profession. Building trust with customers and preserving a good reputation in the workplace both require ethical conduct on the part of businesspeople.

Taking care of your own mental and emotional health is an essential component of self-care. Given that the very nature of therapeutic work can be emotionally taxing, it is absolutely necessary to make self-care a top priority in order to avoid burnout.

Regular Supervision: Even if you are a licensed therapist, you should still consider participating in regular supervision in order to discuss difficult situations, look for support, and make sure your practice is both ethical and effective.

Learning Never Stops: If you want to give your patients the finest care possible, you need to stay current on the most recent research and therapy practices.

Maintaining a Healthy Balance Between Your Personal and Professional Lives In order to keep your general health in good standing, it is imperative that you maintain a healthy balance between your personal and professional lives.

Maintaining Boundaries It is essential for both ethical and effective therapy that therapists continue to hone their skills in establishing and upholding professional boundaries with their clients.

Special Topics and Emerging Trends in Marriage and Family Therapy are Discussed in Chapter 12 of this Book.

The domain of Marriage and Family Therapy (MFT) is an active one that is consistently undergoing new developments. It is essential for a marriage and family therapist (MFT) to remain current on special issues and emerging trends because doing so can help define their practice and improve the quality of service they deliver to clients. In the following chapter, we'll discuss a number of these subjects, including integrated care, teletherapy, cultural competency, and more.

Competence in cultural matters and diversity

The current MFT profession places a significant emphasis on cultural competence as a core competency. In a society that is becoming increasingly varied, it is imperative that therapists have sensitivity to cultural differences and an understanding of how these differences effect the lives and relationships of their clients. The following are important factors to consider:

Develop an understanding of your own cultural assumptions and biases so that you can better communicate with others. Having this level of self-awareness is essential to achieving cultural competency.

Cultivate a mindset of cultural humility by approaching each customer with an attitude that is open, respectful, and inquiring about their distinctive cultural heritage. This will help you build lasting relationships with your customers.

Training in Cultural Competence It is important to seek out training and education on cultural competence. This training and education might take the form of classes, workshops, and reading material that focuses on certain cultural groups and the experiences they have had.

Capacity for Adaptation: Recognize that what is successful in one cultural setting may not be successful in another. Maintain a flexible mindset and be open to making adjustments to your strategy in order to better serve the specific requirements of individual customers.

Collaboration: Work together with experts who come from a variety of professions and cultures to broaden your viewpoint and enhance your capacity to serve a wider range of customers.

Cultural Formulation: Investigate several models of cultural formulation in order to get a deeper understanding of the cultural aspects that influence the difficulties and concerns that clients report.

Electronic therapy and teletherapy

In the field of marriage and family therapy (MFT), teletherapy, often known as e-therapy or online therapy, has become an increasingly important tool. This is especially true in light of the COVID-19 epidemic. This mode of providing services has a few repercussions, including the following:

Accessibility: Teletherapy makes it possible to treat patients who live in rural or otherwise hard-to-reach places. It is a solution for people who might experience geographical or mobility constraints when attempting to obtain therapy.

Ethical Considerations It is imperative that you familiarize yourself thoroughly with the ethical principles and laws pertaining to teletherapy in the jurisdiction in which you practice. This covers concerns regarding technology security, informed consent, and confidentiality of information.

Technical Capability: Familiarize yourself with the hardware and software that is utilized in the process of teletherapy. Get yourself ready to solve any potential technical problems that may crop up during the sessions.

It may be more challenging to establish a strong engagement and rapport in a virtual setting than it would be in traditional face-to-face treatment. Take into consideration several ways to keep in touch with your customers.

Evaluation and Diagnosis: It is vital to modify evaluation and diagnosis procedures so that they can be carried out via teletherapy. Be conscious of the constraints as well as the potential benefits of remote evaluation.

In order to maintain client anonymity during teletherapy sessions, it is important for both you and your clients to ensure that you are in a safe, private setting.

Continuing Education: Through continuing education and professional development, you can ensure that you are always up to date on the most recent findings in teletherapy research, as well as legislation and best practices.

Integrated Health Care and Collaborative Efforts Across Disciplines

The practice of working closely with other members of the medical community as part of an integrated care approach is becoming increasingly common. Here is the information that you require to know:

Approaching Integrated Care Collaboratively Providing Holistic Care for Patients with Complicated Needs is One of the Goals of Integrated Care, Which Involves Close Collaboration With Primary Care Physicians, Psychiatrists, Social Workers, and Other Professionals.

Communication: It is essential for members of the team to effectively communicate with one another and share knowledge. Maintaining customer confidentiality requires the use of secure platforms for the exchange of client information.

Care that Is Centered on the Individual Patient In an environment that provides integrated health care, the primary concern is the health of the individual patient. The members of the team collaborate in order to develop a complete treatment plan that takes the patient's physical, mental, and emotional health into account.

Education and Training: In order to make collaboration with other healthcare professionals easier, you should get familiar with the responsibilities, areas of competence, and ethical rules that govern those areas.

Documentation: Make sure that your documentation is straightforward and to the point so that it is simple for other members of the team to comprehend the background of the client as well as their current standing.

Referrals and Follow-Up: Always be ready to refer clients to other specialists when the situation calls for it, and work closely with those specialists to make sure the client receives the necessary care.

Care that is Sensitive to Trauma

A comprehension of trauma treatment and its application-care that takes into account the possibility that many patients have been through traumatic experiences is absolutely necessary. Among the most important considerations are:

Trauma Sensitivity: Approach every client with sensitivity to the likelihood that they have experienced trauma in the past, and be cognizant of the chance that therapy could result in re-traumatization for the client.

Safety and Trust: Ensure that clients are in a setting that is both safe and trustworthy so that they are comfortable opening up about their experiences.

Clients should be encouraged to take control of their own treatment experience through the use of empowerment techniques. This involves including them in the planning and decision-making processes for their treatment.

Recognizing Triggers It is important to be aware of potential triggers and to respond in a manner that reduces the amount of distress experienced. Clients need to be educated on how to recognize their own triggers.

Self-Care It is important to make regular efforts to practice good self-care in order to avoid experiencing vicarious trauma or burnout. Working with trauma survivors can be an emotionally taxing experience.

Evidence-Based Methods: Investigate trauma treatments supported by evidence, such as Eye Movement Desensitization and Reprocessing (EMDR) and Trauma-Focused Cognitive Behavioral Therapy (TF-CBT).

Practices of Mindfulness and Mind-Body Integration

The benefits of mindfulness and other mind-body activities are increasingly being recognized as valuable components of effective treatment modalities. These methods can assist patients in coping with stress and anxiety, as well as improve their general well-being:

Meditation on Mindfulness Incorporate techniques of meditation on mindfulness to assist clients in becoming more aware of the thoughts, feelings, and physiological sensations that they are experiencing.

Tai Chi and Yoga Mind-body therapies like yoga and tai chi, such as yoga, are good for your physical health and help you relax. They can be especially helpful for individuals who are struggling with issues that are related to stress.

Breathwork is instructing clients on the significance of taking slow, regulated breaths in order to alleviate stress and encourage relaxation.

Mindful Eating: The practices of mindful eating can assist patients in developing a healthier relationship with the food they eat as well as their bodies.

Mindfulness-Based Therapies: Investigate several mindfulness-based therapy techniques, such as Mindfulness-Based Stress Reduction (MBSR) and Mindfulness-Based Cognitive Therapy (MBCT).

Encourage your clients to exercise self-compassion, which entails treating themselves with the same degree of love and understanding that they would offer to a close friend.

Affirmative Therapy for LGBTQ+ Clients

A space that is safe, supportive, and affirming can be created for clients of varying sexual orientations and gender identities through the practice of LGBTQ+ positive therapy. Take into consideration these fundamentals:

Language That Is Inclusive Make sure you use language that is inclusive, and use language that respects and honors the client's sexual orientation and gender identity.

Cultural Competence It is important to have cultural competence in regards to LGBTQ+ issues and to seek additional training if it is required.

Affirming Environment: To ensure that clients feel safe expressing their genuine selves, it is important to cultivate a space that is accepting and affirming.

Recognize that persons who identify as LGBTQ+ have a variety of experiences, some of which are shaped by characteristics such as race, ethnicity, and socioeconomic class. This concept is known as intersectionality.

Support Systems: Assist your clients in constructing robust support systems and navigating the potentially difficult terrain associated with coming out, such as facing discrimination or being rejected.

Being Aware of the influence of Stigma It is important to be aware of the influence that societal stigma and discrimination can have on the mental health and self-esteem of LGBTQ+ clients.

Therapeutic Use of Narratives

Narrative therapy is a client-centered technique that assists individuals in reimagining and rewriting the narratives of their lives. The following are important elements:

Encouraging Clients to regard difficulties as Being Independent from Their Identity Suggest to clients that they regard their difficulties as being independent from their identity. This makes it possible to investigate topics with a greater degree of objectivity.

Reauthoring Narratives include assisting clients in rewriting their life stories in a manner that is congruent with their objectives, core values, and long-term objectives.

Listening and Working Together: Actively listen to the experiences of your customers and work together with them to investigate alternative narratives that enable positive transformation.

Recognize the client as the expert in their own life and story by acknowledging the client's expertise. Your job is to act as a facilitator for the process of reauthoring and exploring new ideas.

Encourage your clients to keep a journal, create artwork, or chronicle their progress in some other creative way so that you can see how far they've come and how their stories have changed.

Treatments based on nature and the environment, such as ecotherapy

Ecotherapy, sometimes known as nature-based therapy, is a relatively new field that acknowledges the therapeutic value of natural environments. This includes the following:

The benefits of spending time in natural environments for enhanced mental health, stress reduction, and overall well-being should be promoted, and this includes time spent connecting with nature.

Outdoor Sessions: If it is possible to do treatment sessions outside, you should strongly consider doing so in order to take advantage of the calming and centering qualities that nature provides.

Metaphors from Nature Encourage your clients to reflect on their own personal development by using images and analogies from the natural world.

Explore the therapeutic benefits of gardening and working with plants as a means of healing and coming into one's own as part of a practice known as horticultural therapy.

Ecopsychology: Dive into the field of ecopsychology, which investigates the connection that exists between humans and the natural world, as well as the ways in which this connection impacts one's mental health.

Emerging Forms of Medical Treatment

Maintain an up-to-date knowledge of new therapy models and approaches being developed in the field of MFT, such as the following:

Emotionally Focused Therapy (EFT) is a type of psychotherapy that aims to enhance the emotional relationships that exist between couples and family members by assisting individuals in more effectively expressing and reacting to their feelings.

Solution-Focused Brief Therapy (SFBT) is a form of therapy that focuses less on problem-solving and more on recognizing and expanding upon potential solutions.

The term "Internal Family Systems" (IFS) refers to a field of study that investigates the inner workings of the mind, identifying distinct subpersonalities and the functions that they play in maintaining emotional health.

Learn about the polyvagal theory and how it can be used in trauma therapy, for the management of the nervous system, and for the improvement of self-regulatory skills.

Approaches Based on Narratives and Postmodern Thought Be on the lookout for postmodern methods of treatment in the field of therapy, including collaborative language systems and social constructionism.

Developments in the State of Technology

The practice of MFT is undergoing a continuous revolution brought on by technological advancements. Take a look at some of these recent developments in technology:

Platforms for Telehealth: If you want to give your customers the most positive experience possible with virtual therapy, make sure you stay current on the newest telehealth platforms and technologies.

Investigate the ways in which artificial intelligence and chatbots are currently being utilized to offer help and services to persons who are dealing with issues related to their mental health.

Apps for Mobile Devices Mindfulness, monitoring one's mood, and accessing resources for self-help are all becoming common uses for mobile applications.

Virtual Reality (VR) treatment: Virtual reality (VR) treatment is becoming increasingly accessible and can be used to treat a number of mental health conditions, including phobias and post-traumatic stress disorder (PTSD).

Online assistance Communities: When working with customers who are looking for peer assistance, it is important to consider the role that online support communities and forums can play.

Self-Care for Future Therapists is Covered in Chapter 13

The path to becoming a marriage and family therapist (MFT) is one that is not only fulfilling but also difficult. You will be exposed to the emotional, psychological, and relational challenges of your clients as you work toward becoming a therapist in the future. You have to make taking care of yourself a top priority if you want to be effective in your work and maintain your own mental and emotional well-being. In this chapter, we will discuss the significance of practicing self-care, the various approaches to practicing self-care, as well as the actionable activities you can take to ensure your continued success in the area of MFT.

The Value of Self-Care for Mental Health Professionals

Self-care is not a luxury; rather, it is an absolute requirement, particularly in the strenuous profession of therapy. The following are some of the reasons why it is essential for aspiring therapists:

The emotional demands of treatment can lead to burnout if they are not managed appropriately, thus it is important to take precautions against this. Burnout can have a negative impact on both your general health and your capacity to give effective therapy to clients.

Keeping an Object Perspective: Practicing good self-care practices will assist you in keeping the required emotional distance and perspective when dealing with clients. Maintaining this mental and emotional equilibrium is essential for successful therapy.

In your function as a therapist, you have the opportunity to serve as a role model for the clients you work with. Clients might be inspired to prioritize their own well-being and given the capacity to do so when self-care methods are demonstrated.

Enhancing Empathy: Practicing self-care allows you to emotionally recharge so that you may continue to be empathetic and compassionate toward your clients, especially during difficult and emotionally intense sessions.

Personal Development Taking care of oneself in healthy ways encourages personal development and self-awareness. As a therapist, you will be able to grow and advance as a result of this opportunity.

Long-Term Viability: If you want your profession to be viable over the long haul, self-care is an absolutely necessary practice. If you don't have it, you run the risk of getting overburdened, exhausted, or disillusioned.

Tips on How Future Counselors Can Take Care of Themselves

A multi-pronged approach is required for effective self-care. It entails paying attention to your physical, emotional, and mental well-being all at the same time. Consider the following options for your next move:

Create Boundaries: Define your professional and personal boundaries in a clear and concise manner. Recognize when it's time to step away from your work and carve out some time exclusively for yourself and the people you care about.

Engage in Mindfulness activities: To alleviate stress and maintain presence of mind, you should engage in mindfulness activities such as meditation and deep breathing exercises.

When you're dealing with difficult issues or ethical conundrums, don't be afraid to seek supervision or consultation; in fact, you shouldn't even think twice about doing so. Support and direction can be gained from having supervision.

Maintaining a support network of friends, family, or coworkers who are able to provide emotional support and encouragement is an important part of staying connected.

Maintaining a regular exercise routine is essential because it is the most effective stress reliever. Include regular exercise as part of your regimen to improve both your state of mind and your level of energy.

Consume a diet that is both well-balanced and diverse in order to maintain and improve your health. Avoid consuming an excessive amount of caffeine and sweets because doing so can cause mood changes.

Adequate Sleep: Make getting decent sleep your top priority. A lack of sleep can have a detrimental effect on your cerebral clarity as well as your emotional fortitude.

Dedicate some of your time each week to the pursuit of hobbies and activities that offer you pleasure and help you unwind. These hobbies are helpful outlets for relieving stress and are recommended.

Take time off for vacations and getaways at regular intervals so that you can refresh your batteries. These breaks are necessary in order for you to maintain a successful career over the long run.

Keeping a Journal It is important to keep a personal journal so that you can reflect on your experiences, feelings, and professional development as a therapist.

Checking in with Yourself on a Regular Basis It is important to check in with yourself on a regular basis in order to evaluate your well-being, stress levels, and emotional state. A healthy dose of self-awareness is an essential component of good self-care.

Continuing Education: If you want to stay abreast of the most recent advancements in your area, you should participate in continuing education and professional development. Your enthusiasm for therapy may be rekindled as a result of this.

Groups of Support You might want to think about joining existing support groups for therapists or starting your own. It might be beneficial to talk to others about your experiences and difficulties.

Practices of self-care that foster emotional toughness

The ability to deal with challenging situations and continue functioning normally in spite of them is referred to as emotional resilience. Because your work as a therapist will bring you into contact with situations that are emotionally intense, cultivating the ability to remain emotionally resilient is essential:

Recognize That It Is alright To Be Vulnerable And Seek Support When You Need It Recognize that it is alright to be vulnerable and seek support when you do. Vulnerability is not a sign of weakness but rather a characteristic shared by all humans.

Enhance your capacity to control your own emotions by working on your emotional regulation skills. Having this ability helps you maintain your composure even when facing challenging situations.

Self-kindness: Make a habit of showing yourself kindness. Apply the same level of compassion and understanding to yourself that you do to your customers and clients.

Finding Healthy Ways to Release Emotions It is important to discover healthy ways to release emotions. This could involve having a conversation with a coworker, indulging in some physical activity, or seeking out psychological help for yourself.

Learn to look at difficult circumstances from a more optimistic perspective by practicing positive reframing. Having this kind of cognitive ability can make you more resilient.

Taking Care of Oneself in Challenging Times

Additional strain may be placed on therapists during difficult times, such as during a pandemic that affects the entire world. Take into consideration the following during these times:

Don't Be Afraid to Ask for Help: If you need help, don't be afraid to ask for it from your coworkers, mentors, or professional groups. You are not the only one dealing with these difficulties.

Adjust Your perform It is important to remember that the environment in which you perform treatment is constantly evolving. Accept teletherapy and maintain your knowledge of its most effective procedures.

Establishing realistic expectations for yourself means acknowledging that there are instances when you may not be able to supply your clients with all the answers or solutions to their problems. The value of support far exceeds that of certainty.

minimize worry and Stress by Managing Your Media Consumption Limiting your exposure to the media can help minimize feelings of worry and stress. Maintain your level of awareness, but try to limit your time spent reading depressing articles.

Recognize That You May Have Your Own challenges Recognize that you may have your own challenges during times that are challenging. It is not a sign of weakness to own your limitations and put your own needs first.

Controlling the Counterflow of Information

The term "countertransference" refers to the emotional emotions of the therapist towards the client. The effective management of countertransference is a crucial component of self-care:

Self-Reflection: Think about the emotional responses you have when interacting with customers. Recognize that these responses might provide insightful information about the therapy process, so keep that in mind.

Consultation: When you become aware of severe countertransference emotions, it is important to seek consultation from a superior or a colleague in order to gain perspective.

Maintain Your Objectivity It is important to guarantee that your emotional reactions do not negatively impact the therapy interaction by maintaining your objectivity and adhering to professional limits at all times.

Supervision: If you have regular supervision, it will be easier for you to analyze countertransference reactions and investigate how such reactions might affect your work.

The Beginnings and the Ends of Things

Transitions in therapy, such as the end of treatment with a client or the beginning of treatment with a new patient, can be difficult on therapists on an emotional level. The following is a guide for navigating these types of situations:

Process of Termination Clients should be prepared for the process of termination, and their feelings about it should be addressed. Give people a sense of closure and encourage them as they make the shift.

Seek supervision in order to address your own feelings about the end of a therapy partnership, and do it in a safe and supportive environment.

Compassion for Oneself It is important to have compassion for oneself when working through the difficult emotional aspects of transitions. Keep in mind that there are inevitable closures associated with the therapeutic process.

Maintaining Professional Boundaries It is important to continue to observe professional boundaries even after a treatment relationship has ended. It is important to refrain from getting too engaged in a client's life outside of the treatment sessions.

The Importance of an Observer in the Process of Self-Care

It is important for therapists to have supervision not only because it is a requirement for their profession but also because it is an effective tool for their own self-care:

Support and Guidance: When you're working through difficult issues or ethical conundrums, having supervision can provide you with the emotional support and guidance you need.

Personal Development You can find areas for both personal and professional development through the process of receiving supervision, which will help you become a more competent therapist.

Emotional Release Make use of supervision as a safe place to process and let go of your own feelings that are connected to the work you do.

Professional Perspective: Supervisors have the ability to offer a more comprehensive viewpoint on your cases, which can assist you in seeing things from a variety of aspects.

Ethical Insights: The opportunity to discuss ethical concerns and dilemmas that arise in the course of your work is provided by supervision. This helps to ensure that you conform to professional rules.

Keeping a Healthy Balance Between Your Personal and Professional Life

Maintaining a healthy equilibrium between your personal and professional lives is a constant struggle for therapists. The following are some techniques that can assist you in preserving this equilibrium:

Establishing firm boundaries requires that you specify your work hours and separate off your personal time. Try not to overcommit yourself to your task.

Time Management: Ensure that you have room in your schedule for self-care and relaxation by practicing efficient time management techniques.

Utilize technology with caution since it has the potential to blur the barrier between your personal life and your business life. Be cautious of how you use it, and establish clear parameters for communication at work.

Communication: Ensure that you keep an open line of communication with the people you care about most regarding your profession and how it may affect your personal life.

Breaks Should Be Scheduled: Breaks and holidays should be scheduled on a regular basis so that you can recharge your batteries and spend quality time with your loved ones.

Practicing Self-Care as a Family You should encourage your family to engage in self-care practices and stress the significance of everyone's overall health and wellness.

Case Studies and Practical Applications in Marriage and Family Therapy are the topics covered in Chapter 14.

In this chapter, we will delve into case studies from the real world and examine practical implementations of the principles and strategies that have been addressed throughout the rest of this study guide. Because marriage and family therapy (MFT) is an ever-evolving subject, it is essential for therapists to be able to tailor their expertise to the specific requirements of each individual client and family. The case studies that are going to be provided here will highlight how concepts from MFT can be implemented in diverse circumstances, and they will also provide insights into the complexities and obstacles that therapists may face.

Case Study No. 1: Restoring Trust in a Marital Relationship

After John confessed to having an extramarital affair, Jane and John, a married couple in their late 30s, decided to seek counseling. The affair had destroyed Jane's trust, and as a result, the couple was on the verge of splitting up.

Application: The therapist started by addressing Jane's feelings of betrayal and John's regret as the first step in the healing process. They attended counseling sessions both individually and as a couple in order to investigate the factors that contributed to the affair, such as a breakdown in communication and unfulfilled emotional needs. Emotionally Focused Therapy (EFT) was utilized by the therapist in order to assist the couple in communicating their thoughts, feelings, and requirements in an open and honest manner, so promoting feelings of empathy and comprehension between the two parties. Active listening and emotional attunement were both skills that needed to be practiced, so homework assignments were assigned. Trust was reestablished between the couple as time went on, and they became better able to communicate with one another and satisfy each other's emotional need.

Case Study 2: Conflict Between Parents and Children

Context: Sarah, who is 15 years old, was brought to therapy by her parents because of the intensifying tensions that were occurring at home. She became more stubborn as time went on, and she distanced herself more and further from her family.

Application: The therapist utilized strategies from story Therapy in order to assist Sarah in externalizing her problems and rewriting the story she had been telling herself. They encouraged Sarah to share her viewpoint and thoughts in a way that was non-confrontational and listened to her. In order to facilitate better communication and acquire a more in-depth grasp of Sarah's requirements, the therapist included the parents in the sessions. Sarah was able to come away from this experience with a sense of having been heard, and her parents gained the ability to establish clear boundaries and penalties. The fights became less frequent, which led to an overall improvement in the family dynamic.

Challenges Facing Blended Families (Case Study No. 3)

Context: Mark and Emily had only recently remarried, which resulted in the formation of a blended family with all of their previous children. They were having a difficult time dealing with competition, animosity, and contention among the step-siblings.

Application: The therapist's primary focus was on creating a secure yet welcoming environment within which all members of the family could freely discuss their thoughts, feelings, and concerns. In order to reorganize the dynamics of the family and make roles and boundaries more clear, they utilized the structural family therapy procedures. The therapist did her best to cultivate empathy among the step-siblings by facilitating open conversations about their emotions and encouraging the step-siblings to participate in activities together. After some time had passed, the dynamics within the family began to improve, and they became better able to negotiate the intricacies of their blended family via increased collaboration and understanding.

Grief and loss in a family unit: the fourth case study

The Rodriguez family suffered a devastating loss when their oldest son was killed in an accident, and as a result, they are fighting to find a way to cope with their grief.

Application: The therapist utilized techniques from sorrow Therapy in order to assist each member of the family in processing their sorrow on an individual level while also bringing the family members together to discuss their memories and feelings. They did something special as a family to remember and honor the life of the deceased son. The therapist highlighted how important it is to give each member of the family the space and time they need to grieve in their own individual ways and at their own pace. The passing of time allowed the family to begin the process of healing, and the shared experience of mourning brought them closer together as they honored the memory of their son.

Case Study No. 5: Dependency and Substance Abuse

Emily's husband, David, enabled her addiction by providing financial and emotional support despite the damage it caused to their relationship. Emily was battling with substance misuse, and David enabled her addiction by providing financial and emotional support.

In order to treat Emily's addiction and David's codependent behavior, the therapist implemented strategies from the field of substance abuse therapy (SAT). They worked on both their own and with their partners in separate and combined sessions. Emily was given resources to assist her in her recovery from addiction, while David received education on codependency and learned how to establish good boundaries. The therapist prompted them to discuss their feelings and requirements in an open and honest manner. Emily's rehabilitation improved over time, and David's codependent behaviors became less severe as they worked together to reconstruct their relationship on more independent terms.

Case Study No. 6: Young People Who Are Depressed

Jake, who was 16 years old at the time, was brought to therapy by his parents owing to the extreme sadness he was experiencing. He had been having trouble at school, which had led to him being socially isolated, and he had also lost interest in the hobbies he had enjoyed.

Application: The therapist made use of techniques from cognitive behavioral therapy (CBT) in order to assist Jake in recognizing unhealthy thought patterns and creating new ones that are more beneficial. They built a home environment that was supportive of Jake and encouraged him to participate in things he had previously enjoyed. Additionally, any potential underlying issues that could be contributing to Jake's depression were investigated by the therapist. Jake's symptoms began to improve over the course of time, and he eventually reclaimed his sense of purpose and pleasure.

Case Study No. 7: Getting Over a Traumatic Experience

Background: Laura, now 40 years old, had suffered traumatic events as a youngster, which continued to have an impact on her relationships, self-esteem, and overall well-being even into adulthood.

Application: The therapist utilized techniques from Trauma-Informed Therapy in order to establish a secure and comforting atmosphere for Laura so that she could work through the trauma that she had experienced. They decided to use a treatment called Eye Movement Desensitization and Reprocessing (EMDR) in order to assist Laura in reprocessing the terrible memories she had. In order to empower Laura along her path to recovery, the therapist placed a strong emphasis on self-compassion and practices of self-care. The symptoms of trauma that Laura was experiencing reduced with time, and she gained a sense of control over her life as well as emotional well-being.

Case Study No. 8: Variations in Cultural Marriage Practices

Context: Maria, who is Latina, and John, who is Caucasian, encountered difficulties in their marriage as a result of the cultural disparities and expectations between their two groups.

Application: The therapist utilized strategies from the book "Cultural Competence in Therapy" in order to investigate how the clients' different cultural backgrounds affected their relationship. They promoted open conversations regarding the cultural backgrounds, values, and expectations of each relationship. The therapist assisted the couple in recognizing the value of the richness of their varied backgrounds as well as finding areas of common ground. Maria and John's relationship flourished as they became able to appreciate and benefit from the unique aspects of each other's cultures over time.

Study No. 9: Affirmative Therapy for LGBTQ+ Clients

Context: Alex, a non-binary person, decided to seek therapy in order to receive help with regard to their gender identification and the challenges they were experiencing within their family.

Application: In order to provide Alex with an affirming and supportive environment, the therapist utilized several approaches from the LGBTQ+ Affirmative Therapy model. They assisted Alex in figuring out their gender identity, coming to terms with the disapproval of their family, and developing a robust support network within the LGBTQ+ community. Alex eventually became more self-accepting and resilient, and they discovered that their identity gave them a source of strength.

Case Study No. 10: Elderly Care and the Role of Family Caregivers

Context: While providing care for their elderly parents, the Johnson family struggled with a number of difficulties. There were disagreements on who was responsible for providing care for their parents and who was concerned about how their parents were doing.

Application: In order to address the dynamics of the family and the responsibilities that each member plays, the therapist utilized approaches from family systems therapy. They devised a strategy to divide up the caregiving obligations and encouraged open conversation about the difficulties of providing care. The therapist highlighted the significance of self-care for those who provided care for their family members. The family has, over the course of time, built a system for caregiving that is more organized and helpful. This has resulted in fewer arguments and an overall improvement in the health of their elderly parents.

The process of obtaining a license to practice marriage and family therapy is discussed in Chapter 15. This chapter also covers professional development.

To embark on the path to becoming a Licensed Marriage and Family Therapist (LMFT), one must first go on an extensive journey of professional development before satisfying certain licensure requirements. As you work toward becoming a licensed MFT, there are a number of steps and factors that need to be taken into consideration. In this chapter, we will walk you through those steps and factors. In this lesson, we are going to discuss the educational requirements, supervised experience requirements, licensure exam requirements, and ongoing professional development needs.

Educational Prerequisites and Obligations

A master's degree in Marriage and Family Therapy or a field that is very closely related is often required to become a Licensed Marriage and Family Therapist (LMFT). Listed below are the most important educational prerequisites:

Bachelor's Degree: To begin, you should get a Bachelor's degree in an area connected to psychology, such as counseling, social work, or psychology. Make sure that the classes you took during your undergraduate studies are compatible with the requirements for master's degree programs in marriage and family therapy (MFT).

Master's Degree: Complete a training program that has been approved by the Commission on Accreditation for Marriage and Family Therapy Education (COAMFTE) in order to earn a Master's degree in Marriage and Family Therapy. A degree in a similar discipline, such as psychology or social work, may also be accepted in certain states.

Your Master's program will involve coursework on the theory, practices, ethics, and intercultural aspects of marriage and family therapy (MFT). In addition, as a part of your curriculum, you will participate in supervised clinical training.

Clinical Hours: Be ready to amass a predetermined amount of supervised clinical hours in accordance with the requirements set forth by the licensing board in your state. During the course of your Master's program, you will normally accumulate these hours.

Internship: As part of the Master's degree requirements, you will be required to complete either an internship or a practicum, which will give you hands-on experience while being supervised.

Thesis or Capstone: Certain schools call for the completion of a thesis or capstone project, which typically entails conducting original research or an in-depth investigation of a specific case.

Counseling abilities During the course of your educational journey, you should work on developing good counseling and communication abilities. These abilities are absolutely necessary for a successful career as an MFT.

Experience That Is Supervised

After you have finished all of the educational requirements that are required of you, the next step in the process of getting your license will be to collect supervised work experience:

Supervised Clinical Hours: In order to become licensed in most jurisdictions, you are required to complete a certain number of supervised clinical hours. This quantity varies from state to state but is often between 2,000 and 4,000 hours. These hours must be earned after the completion of a master's degree and are often obtained through postgraduate employment or participation in an internship.

Work under the supervision of a certified marriage and family therapist (MFT) or another trained mental health professional who has been approved by the licensing board in your state.

Meetings with Your Supervisor You are required to meet with your supervisor on a regular basis in order to review your cases, obtain comments, and check that you are meeting the requirements for licensing.

Direct Client Contact: You are required to have direct client contact for a predetermined portion of your supervised hours. During this time, you are to deliver therapy services to your patients.

customer base: Certain states have unique regulations pertaining to the diversity of your customer base, and these regulations must be followed. Be aware of these requirements, and make it a priority to obtain experience working with a variety of different types of customers.

Documentation of Supervision It is imperative that you keep detailed documentation of your supervised experience. This documentation should include case notes, supervision agreements, and supervision summaries. The body that oversees licensing in your state might take a look at these documents.

Examens de Licenciatura

You will need to obtain a passing score on a licensing examination that is particular to your state in order to work as an LMFT. Typical questions on tests are:

Exam: The MFT nationwide Examination is a nationwide exam that is offered by the Association of Marital and Family Therapy Regulatory Boards (AMFTRB). In many states, obtaining a license to practice requires first obtaining a passing score on this examination. Your knowledge of MFT theory, practices, and ethical standards will be evaluated using this test.

Exam for the State: In addition to or as a replacement for the national exam, several states administer their very own exam for licensure. You should get in touch with the licensing board in your state to find out which exam(s) you need to pass.

Exam Preparation In order to be prepared for these exams, you will likely need to study MFT theory and practice, in addition to researching ethical rules and regulations that are particular to your state. You can improve your chances of success by making use of the study materials and preparation classes that are available to you.

Application for license After you have successfully completed all of the necessary examinations, you must then submit an application for license to the licensing board in your state. Be sure to have your transcripts, a proof of supervised experience, your test scores, and any other evidence that may be requested on hand.

Improvement of One's Profession in Addition to Ongoing Education

Your journey of professional development does not come to an end once you become a licensed marriage and family therapist (LMFT). For the purpose of keeping your license current and remaining knowledgeable in your field, continuing education is absolutely necessary. Here is the information that you require to know:

Continuing Education Requirements The majority of states mandate that licensed marriage and family therapists (LMFTs) accumulate a specified number of continuing education units (CEUs) before their licenses can be renewed. Workshops, seminars, conferences, and even online courses can all help you earn continuing education units (CEUs).

Ethical and Legal Updates: Make sure you are up to current on any alterations that have been made to the ethical norms, legislation, and regulations that are associated with MFT in your state. Infractions of ethical standards might result in disciplinary actions and put your license in jeopardy.

Specialization and Advanced Training: If you want to improve your talents and the options available to you in the job market, you should seriously consider obtaining certifications or specializing training in a field such as addiction counseling, trauma therapy, or LGBTQ+ affirmative therapy.

Memberships in Professional Organizations Become a member of a professional organization such as the American Association for Marriage and Family Therapy (AAMFT) to gain access to resources, opportunity to network with other professionals, and support for your professional development.

Supervision and Mentorship: In order to support novice therapists in their professional growth, some LMFTs choose to take on the role of supervisor or mentor. This is a facet of professional development that may result in gratifying experiences.

Keeping Current: Ensure that you are up to date on all of the most recent research, therapy practices, and emerging trends in the industry. Participate at conferences, educate yourself with relevant literature, and have meaningful conversations with your peers.

Upholding Ethical Standards of Conduct

The MFT profession places a premium on ethical behavior in the treatment of clients. The following are some fundamental tenets that should be upheld:

Respect and safeguard the confidentiality of client information, only violating it when forced to do so by law or where there is a threat to the client's well-being.

Obtaining Informed Consent From Patients It is important to obtain informed consent from patients by first outlining the nature and purpose of therapy, along with any potential risks and patient rights.

Establishing distinct professional boundaries with customers helps you steer clear of parallel relationships as well as potential conflicts of interest.

Cultural Competence It is important to make every effort to be culturally competent and to give care that is both affirming and objective to patients who come from a wide variety of backgrounds.

Client Autonomy: When it comes to making decisions about their own life and therapy goals, clients should be respected and given support for their autonomy.

Avoid Causing Harm: You should take precautions so that the actions you take do not put your customers in danger. Always be aware of the possibility for damage, and take measures to protect yourself from it.

Conflict of Interest: It is important to be open and honest about any possible conflicts of interest, and you should put the satisfaction of your customers ahead of your own financial gain.

Maintaining a Professional Attitude It is imperative to always have an upstanding professional attitude when interacting with clients, coworkers, and other stakeholders.

Problems of a Legal and Ethical Nature

Challenges of a legal and ethical nature may await you if you choose to work in the field of MFT. To navigate these challenges in a careful and professional manner is absolutely necessary. The following are some examples of common difficulties:

Reporting Obligations: It is important that you get familiar with the rules governing reporting obligations in your state. In some circumstances, such as when a kid or an elderly person is being abused, you could be required by law to make a report.

Breaches of Confidentiality Violating a client's right to privacy, whether unintentionally or on purpose, can result in legal and ethical repercussions. Put in place robust protections for your personal information, and be extra careful to avoid compromising confidentially.

Protecting the Interests of Your Customers: Put the safety and happiness of your customers first. If you have reason to fear that one of your customers is going to hurt themselves or someone else, you must take the necessary precautions to protect them.

Dual Relationships: You should exercise extreme caution when engaging in dual relationships, which occur when you have a personal relationship in addition to a business one with a customer. These can give rise to ethical conflicts, which require cautious management on your part.

Violations of limits It is crucial to keep clear limits at all times. Crossing a boundary without permission might result in ethical complaints and put your license at risk.

Consent to Treatment Always make sure to have clients' informed consent before initiating any kind of treatment. Describe the nature of the treatment, its goals, and any possible adverse effects.

Insurance for Businesses and Professionals

Having professional liability insurance is something that is strongly advised for you to do. If you have this insurance, you will be protected in the event that your therapy practice is subject to any legal claims or litigation. In the event that legal action is taken against you, this insurance policy will pay for your legal defense as well as any potential settlements. As a result, your personal financial burden will be reduced.

Interactive Resources and Study Groups for the Master of Family Therapy Examination Chapter 16

The process of getting ready for the Marriage and Family Therapy (MFT) exam can be one that is both difficult and time-consuming. Think about participating in study groups or using interactive resources to improve your level of preparation and increase your odds of being successful. In this chapter, we will discuss a variety of platforms, tools, and tactics that can make your exam preparation more efficient while also keeping your interest levels high.

The Potential of Using Interactive Materials

Because they force you to participate actively in the process of learning, interactive resources are a very useful tool for MFT exam preparation. They can assist you in improving your critical thinking skills, expanding your knowledge base, and bolstering your self-assurance. Consider utilizing some of the following interactive resources:

1. Mock tests taken via the internet

The use of online practice examinations is one of the most important resources that should be utilized when studying for the MFT exam. They replicate the format and organization of the real exam, giving you a sense of the kinds of questions you'll be asked as well as the time limits you'll be under during the test. Try to find practice tests that have been developed by respected organizations or test preparation agencies, as the material on these tests is more likely to mirror that which will be found on the actual exam.

2. a deck of flashcards

Studying key terminology, concepts, and meanings can be accomplished effectively with the use of flashcards. They are especially helpful for memory and bringing information to mind quickly. You have the option of either creating flashcards physically or using digital flashcard platforms and apps such as Quizlet or Anki.

3. Guides to Studying That Are Interactive

Study guides that are interactive mix traditional text-based material with interactive components such as quizzes, films, and other forms of multimedia content. These guides make your study time more interesting and provide a range of different techniques to help you solidify your comprehension of the material.

4. Mobile applications

There are apps available for mobile devices that are created expressly for the purpose of MFT exam preparation. The majority of the time, these apps feature study timetables, flashcards, and practice questions. AATBS, Therapy Exam Prep, and MFT Exam Pro are three well-known mobile applications that can be used to prepare for the MFT exam.

5. Study Groups That Take Place Online

Participants in the MFT test can gather together in virtual study groups, which are online communities or platforms, to talk about various topics, ask questions about them, and share resources. They can assist you obtain alternative perspectives on the subject that will be on the exam and provide a supportive setting in which peer learning can take place.

6. Online Video Presentations and Live Webinars

Learning can be accomplished through both sight and sound with the help of video lectures and webinars. These tools could be made available to you by companies that specialize in test preparation or by teachers who have extensive experience in MFT exam preparation. They have the ability to assist you in comprehending difficult ideas and providing you with explanations from experts.

7. Online Communities, Forums, and Message Boards

You can ask questions, get advice, and share your experiences with others who are also preparing for the exam by participating in online forums and discussion boards, such as those that can be found on Reddit or on specialist websites devoted to MFT exam preparation.

Organizing an Effective Study Group for Students

When it comes to the preparation for the MFT exam, study groups can be an extremely useful instrument. They not only give inspiration and a network of support, but also make it possible for you to gain access to the collective wisdom and perspectives of your contemporaries. The following are some steps that can be taken to form and maintain a productive study group:

1. Seek Out Peers Who Share Your Values

Find other people who are getting ready for the MFT exam and are dedicated to the accomplishments of the study group as a whole. Consider potential applicants that have a variety of skills and expertise in a variety of MFT-related areas.

2. Clarify Both Your Objectives and Expectations

Concisely define the study group's objectives and requirements for participation. Which particular subjects will you be discussing? How frequently do you plan to get together? In what fashion will the studying sessions be conducted?

3. Pick a System for Holding Meetings

Determine the format that will be used for the meetings of your study group. There are a variety of options available, such as social networking platforms, websites dedicated specifically to study groups, and video conferencing applications such as Zoom, Google Meet, or Microsoft Teams.

4. Make a timetable for your studies.

Make a study calendar that includes the topics that are going to be covered in each session as well as the goals that are going to be accomplished during each session. Be careful to schedule enough time in your schedule for studying and taking mock examinations.

5. Use division to get victory.

Put different members of the group in charge of particular subjects or fields of research based on the areas in which they excel. After that, each participant can either make a presentation on the topic allocated to them or conduct a discussion on the subject.

6. Take an active role in the process

Participate in an energetic manner in the sessions of the study group. In this topic, you are encouraged to add your knowledge, ask questions, and take part in the conversation. It may be beneficial to take turns moderating sessions in order to guarantee that the conversation remains even-keeled and fruitful.

7. Pool Your Available Resources

It would be helpful if you could share relevant resources with one another, such as sample tests, flashcards, study guides, and books. Develop a collection of useful resources for the entire membership through cooperative curation of a library.

8. Establish Criteria for Accountability

Establish metrics of accountability to ensure that members are maintaining their progress toward their intended levels of academic achievement. This may involve committing to do certain chores or checking in on their progress at regular intervals.

9. Have an appreciation for the many different learning styles.

Recognize that different members of the group may have varying interests and approaches to learning. While some people learn more from participating in group conversations, others are more motivated by working on their own. Maintain a flexible attitude in order to accommodate varied approaches.

10. Give them support on an emotional level

Getting ready for a test with a lot riding on it can be a stressful experience. Provide members of the group with the emotional support they need by empathizing with the difficulties they are experiencing, offering words of encouragement, and encouraging one another to have a healthy work-life balance.

11. Get experience by taking simulated tests.

Include mock examinations in the times that you spend studying in groups. Review the questions together and discuss the reasons behind correct and incorrect responses.

12. Take a Look Back and Think About It

After each session, you should set aside some time to go over the material that was presented and evaluate your progress. Determine the topics on which you will need to spend more time reading, and adapt your study schedule accordingly.

Platforms and Resources for Online Research and Instruction

Participants in the MFT exam have access to a number of online platforms and tools that have been created with the express purpose of assisting them in their preparation:

AATBS, which stands for the Association for Advanced Training in the Behavioral Sciences, is a company that provides extensive preparation tools for the MFT exam. These products include study packages, practice exams, and online workshops.

This online resource, which is part of the Therapist Development Center, offers structured study schedules as well as practice tests. It is well-known for the successful test-taking tactics it offers as well as the help it provides from qualified therapists.

AMFTRB stands for the Association of Marital and Family Therapy Regulatory Boards. The website of the AMFTRB, which is the official website, includes information about the MFT national test as well as a practice exam.

Quizlet is a website that allows users to contribute flashcards, study sets, and quizzes. These materials are prepared by people who have already passed the MFT exam. It is a useful resource for conducting a speedy evaluation.

This website provides extensive study resources and mock exams that are tailored to the subject of the MFT California Clinical Exam, which you will need to take in order to become a licensed marriage and family therapist in the state of California.

MFT Study Guide: This website includes free study resources, such as flashcards, practice exams, and study recommendations for individuals who are going to be taking the MFT exam.

MFT Connect is an online community and study group platform designed specifically for the purpose of preparing for the MFT exam. It enables you to connect with other students, talk about subjects related to the exam, and share information.

Keeping Oneself Motivated and Organized

Getting ready for the MFT exam is a process that takes a long time and calls for organization and motivation. Here are some pointers that will assist you in maintaining your progress:

Define Your Goals and Create a Study Plan: Define your goals and create a study plan that specifies what you need to cover and when you plan to take the exam. Set Clear Objectives.

Make Use of a Study timetable: Make a study timetable for yourself, allocating particular amounts of time to certain areas of study. Maintain as close an adherence to this schedule as you possibly can.

Maintain a Record of Your Progress: In order to keep a record of your progress, you should maintain a record of the topics that you have covered as well as the areas that require more attention.

Regular Practice It is important to practice on a regular basis, including practice tests and review questions. This not only tests your knowledge but also gets you accustomed to the layout of the exam so that you may perform better on it.

Hold Yourself Accountable Discuss your objectives with a close friend or member of your family who is able to assist you in holding yourself accountable for your study obligations.

Reward Yourself You should celebrate your accomplishments by creating a reward system for yourself. After you've finished a particularly taxing study session, for instance, give yourself a reward that you enjoy doing.

To keep your body and mind in good shape, it's important to keep a balanced lifestyle by making sure you receive enough sleep, exercise, and a healthy diet. Take breaks at regular intervals to protect yourself from burnout.

Imagine yourself succeeding: Visualization can be an extremely useful technique. Imagine passing the test with flying colors and achieving your goal of being a licensed MFT. Devote some time each day to this mental exercise.

Maintain Your Knowledge: Make sure you keep up with the latest information regarding the MFT exam, such as changes in the testing methods or the content of the exam.

Participate in Peer Support Groups: Talk to other people who are getting ready for the test at the same time as you do. When you are confronted with difficulties, they are able to supply you with helpful insights and motivate you.

Preparing for the California Jurisprudence Examination is Covered in Chapter 17

As part of the requirements for obtaining a license to practice as a Marriage and Family Therapist (MFT) in the state of California, you will have to pass the California Jurisprudence Exam. This test is given as part of the licensing procedure. The purpose of this specialized test is to evaluate your knowledge of the statutes and rules that regulate the practice of MFT in the state of California. In this chapter, we will delve into the intricacies of the California Jurisprudence Exam, offering assistance on how to prepare for and succeed in this important step toward becoming a qualified MFT in the state of California. This exam is one of the requirements for becoming a licensed MFT in the state of California.

Comprehending the Jurisprudence Test for the State of California

The purpose of the California Jurisprudence Exam, which is a state-specific test, is to determine whether or not you have a sufficient awareness of the legal and ethical norms that regulate the practice of marriage and family therapy in the state of California. The laws, regulations, and professional standards that are relevant to your work are the primary emphasis of this section. The following is an outline of the most important information regarding the test:

1. Content that is Unique to the State The California Jurispru districts Exam tests a candidate' Tribunal's knowledge of regulations that are unique to the state of California and may be different from those in other states.

2. Test Conducted Via Computer In most cases, the examination will be conducted in the form of a computerized test at one of the authorized testing locations. In order to take the exam, you will need to schedule a time slot in advance.

3. The amount of questions on the examination varies, and they are typically presented in a multiple-choice format. The number of questions on the exam is subject to change, and the California Board of Behavioral Sciences (BBS) decides what the minimum score must be to pass.

4. Content Categories The examination covers a wide variety of content categories, some of which are legal and ethical standards, reporting obligations, confidentiality, the area of practice, and client rights. There is a possibility that the questions will be scenario-based, challenging you to apply your knowledge to various predicaments.

5. Payment of the Exam Fee In order to register for the California Jurisprudence Exam, you will be needed to pay the examination fee. The California Board of Behavioral Sciences will charge you this amount in addition to the fees for the application and the license that you must pay.

Studying for the Jurisprudence Examination for the State of California

To be successful on the California Jurisprudence Exam, preparation is absolutely necessary. To assist you in getting ready, the following is a step-by-step guide:

1. Read through the Student Handbook.

An approved study guide can be obtained from the California Board of Behavioral Sciences in order to prepare for the California Jurisprudence Exam. You should begin by reading this guide, which provides an overview of the subject matter areas that will be tested, the format of the exam, and the policies and procedures that you are required to be familiar with. The guide is available on the BBS website.

2. Familiarize yourself with the laws and regulations of California

Spend some time familiarizing yourself with the rules and regulations that govern the practice of marriage and family therapy in the state of California. The Business and Professions Code as well as the California Code of Regulations are the two primary sources that were used to compile this information. Pay particular attention to the legislation that pertain to your area of activity, the confidentiality of your clients, and the norms of ethics.

3. Get Your Hands On Some Reading Material

There is a wide variety of reading material at your disposal to assist you in getting ready for the California Jurisprudence Exam. Think about making use of these many resources:

Official Study Guide of the BBS The California Board of Legal Specialization (BBS) offers a study guide that is tailored to the Jurisprudence Exam. This study guide provides you with helpful insights as well as practice questions to assist you in preparing.

Books: Books that cover California MFT law and ethics might be an extremely useful resource. Search for resources that are specifically focused on the regulations of California.

Courses Taken Via the Internet: MFT candidates can choose from a variety of courses taken via the internet to better prepare for the California Jurisprudence Exam. Video lectures, practice questions, and other forms of interactive information are frequently included in these classes.

Exam Simulations: Search for simulations of the format used on the California Jurisprudence Exam when looking for practice examinations. These can assist you in becoming accustomed to the various types of questions that you will be asked.

Flashcards: If you want to learn important phrases, concepts, and legal provisions, you should use flashcards. Making your own flashcards and using them as a study tool can be quite helpful.

4. Construct a Learning Strategy

Make a study plan that includes your study schedule, the subjects that you will cover on a daily or weekly basis, and any practice tests that you will take. Be honest with yourself about how much time you can devote to studying, and do your best to follow the schedule you create for yourself.

5. Put Yourself to the Test

Practice tests should be used on a regular basis to check both your current knowledge and your development. Examine your performance and go back over the questions you got wrong and learn from your mistakes. This will assist you in determining the areas of study on which you ought to concentrate your efforts.

6. Seek Out Assistance

You should seriously consider reaching out to colleagues or mentors who have previously passed the California Jurisprudence Exam for the purpose of receiving advice and direction from them. They are able to provide wisdom and discuss the experiences they've had.

7. Remember to take breaks and deal with your stress.

Putting in the effort to prepare for an important test might be stressful. Make sure that you are taking breaks on a consistent basis, that you are managing your stress, and that you are keeping a healthy work-life balance. It is possible that overscheduling your study time will not produce the desired results.

8. Conduct an examination of the Ethical and Legal Standards

Conduct a comprehensive analysis of the ethical and legal criteria that are unique to marriage and family therapy. It is important that you are aware of the rights of your clients, the confidentiality of their information, the reporting requirements, and the scope of your activity as specified by California law.

9. Put Your Skills and Knowledge into Practice

There is a possibility that you will be asked scenario-based questions on the California Jurisprudence Exam. These questions will require you to apply the knowledge you have gained to actual-life scenarios. Putting this into practice means having conversations about hypothetical case scenarios with your coworkers or mentors.

10. Keep Yourself Up to Date

Maintain an awareness of the most recent amendments and revisions to the rules and regulations governing the practice of MFT in the state of California. The website of the BBS is a very helpful resource for keeping up to date.

Organizing Your Study Time and Taking the Test

As soon as you feel that you have achieved an appropriate level of preparation, it is time to make arrangements to take the California Jurisprudence Exam. Here is the information that you require to know:

1. Scheduling: To arrange your exam, either visit the website of the California BBS or get in touch with the BBS directly. When you schedule your exam, you will be required to pay the examination fee.

2. Identification: On the day of the exam, you are required to present a legitimate form of identification issued by the government, such as a driver's license or a passport.

3. Exam Center: You will be required to take the exam at a testing center that has been approved. Check that you are familiar with both the location and the address of the center.

4. The format of the exam contains of multiple-choice questions and is often administered on a computer. This is the California Jurisprudence Exam. There is flexibility in both the format and the amount of questions.

5. The Results: When you have finished the test, you will then be given the results. If you are successful, you will be able to move on to the subsequent stages of getting your license. If you don't pass the test the first time, you can take it again, but you might have to wait a certain amount of time before doing so.

Staying Informed: Legal and Ethical Updates for Marriage and Family Therapists is the Topic of Chapter 18, which is Available Now!

Keeping up with the latest developments in legal and ethical standards is of the utmost importance in the fast-paced profession of marriage and family therapy (MFT). As a Marriage and Family Therapist (MFT), maintaining compliance with ever-evolving legal and ethical standards is not only your obligation but also a requirement. In this chapter, we will discuss the importance of keeping up to date with these changes, the resources that may be relied on, and the ways in which you can incorporate the latest ethical and legal developments into your practice.

The Importance of Keeping Up to Date with Legal and Ethical Changes

Client Welfare: The client's rights and welfare are intended to be protected by the legal and ethical standards that have been established. Keeping up with current events enables you to give the best possible care and keep the confidence of the people you serve.

The requirement to stay current with new information stems from one's professional responsibility. In the MFT area, this is an essential component of the professional duty that one must uphold.

Risk Management: Keeping up with changes in ethical standards and the law is an effective way to reduce the likelihood that you may be accused of malpractice, receive complaints, or face legal action.

Maintaining your understanding of legal and ethical norms is essential if you want to have a long and fruitful career as a marriage and family therapist (MFT). Your professional future and license could be at risk if you do not comply with the regulations.

Care Quality Having knowledge that is up to date enables you to give care of a higher quality and to make judgments that are more informed when faced with challenging scenarios.

Updates on the Law and Ethics from the Following Sources

Consider the following sources in order to keep up with the latest developments in ethical and legal matters:

Organizations such as the American Association for Marriage and Family Therapy (AAMFT) and the American Psychological Association (APA) are examples of professional organizations that offer resources, publications, and updates on legal and ethical issues.

Your state licensing board is a main source for state-specific legal and ethical updates, and it is important that you stay in good standing with them. They frequently supply things like announcements, advice materials, and newsletters.

Participate in MFT-related workshops, seminars, and conferences as part of your continuing education to gain access to the most recent knowledge regarding legal and ethical standards.

Online resources such as websites, forums, and blogs that are focused on MFT frequently offer updates, discussions, and case studies linked to topics of legal and ethical concern.

Peer Discussions: Participating in conversations with one's peers, including one's coworkers, bosses, and mentors, is an efficient approach to share information and keep oneself informed.

Implementing the Latest Legal and Ethical Developments in Practice

Review on a Regular Basis: Make sure that you leave room in your schedule to conduct regular evaluations of relevant legal and ethical standards. Establish a regular pattern in which you check the websites and publications that are relevant.

Documentation: Ensure that you document all of your interactions with clients in a way that is both clear and complete, conforming to the most recent legal and ethical requirements. In the event of a complaint or legal action, having this documentation on hand can be of critical importance.

guidance: When confronted with difficult ethical conundrums, it is important to seek guidance from one's peers or superiors. Better choices can result from having conversations about specific circumstances and considering a variety of points of view.

Continuing Education: If you want to learn more about ethical and legal issues, you should enroll in continuing education classes. The renewal of a license in many states necessitates the completion of continuing education in several fields.

Client Education It is important to educate your clients on their legal rights, the nature of therapy, the importance of maintaining confidentiality, and the steps involved in the therapeutic process. Clients who are well-informed are more likely to participate fully in the therapeutic process.

Supervision: If you are in a position of supervision, it is your responsibility to advise supervisees on the most recent ethical and legal norms. Make sure that they are practicing in accordance with these guidelines.

Updates on the Most Common Legal and Ethical Issues

Teletherapy Regulations: Make sure you are up to date on the legal requirements for delivering teletherapy services, particularly in light of the expansion of online counseling.

Understanding the most recent interpretations of confidentiality laws and exceptions, including when and how to break confidentiality when it is appropriate, is essential for maintaining secrecy.

Informed Consent It is important to go over the components of informed consent and make sure that clients are aware of the nature of therapy, its objectives, the possible dangers involved, and their rights.

Client Rights: It is important to stay up to speed on the latest information regarding the rights of clients, which include the clients' rights to autonomy and self-determination, as well as their freedom to decline or end therapy.

Dual Relationships: It is important to have a solid understanding of the complexities involved in dual relationships and be able to deftly handle tricky scenarios in which you may find yourself in a personal or other non-business related relationship with a customer.

Maintaining a current knowledge of best practices for cultural competence and offering therapy that is sensitive to other cultures requires cultural competence. Consider enrolling in a course that focuses on diversity and inclusion.

Awareness of the Ethical Implications of keeping an Online Presence It is important to be aware of the ethical implications of keeping an online presence. This includes being aware of how you display yourself on social media and on your website.

Professional Boundaries: Always be on the lookout for ways to violate ethical standards in your interactions with clients and steer clear of any activities or connections that could put your reputation in jeopardy.

Applying the Latest Legal and Ethical Developments to Case Studies

Let's look at some real-world examples to see how recent ethical and legal developments can be applied:

Case Study Number One: Compliance with Teletherapy

A licensed marriage and family therapist has recently begun providing services via teletherapy. They do not have a clear understanding of the ethical and regulatory conditions that must be met for teletherapy.

In the application process, the therapist checks with the state licensing board for the most recent regulations concerning teletherapy. They ensure that the platforms they are employing are both safe and compatible with HIPAA, they acquire clients' informed consent before engaging in teletherapy, and they are aware of any limits that may be imposed on the provision of services across state boundaries.

Case Study No. 2: Privacy Concerns and Potential Dangers

Context: A therapist is working with a client who has revealed that they have had thoughts of hurting themselves. The therapist is worried about striking a balance between the client's privacy and their own protection.

Application: The therapist is aware of the legal exceptions to confidentiality that apply in situations where the client poses a risk to themselves or to others. They have a conversation about this with the customer and come up with a safety strategy together. The therapist takes notes on the conversations that take place and records their decision regarding whether or not to respect client confidentiality.

The Dual Relationship (Case Study No. 3) The Catch-22

Context: A therapist's cousin is interested in receiving therapy, which could lead to the formation of a dual relationship.

In this application, the therapist will investigate the moral standards and legal requirements associated with dual relationships. They come to the conclusion that they should confer with a supervisor and talk to the relative about the matter. If they decide to continue therapy, they make certain to set clear boundaries and document the arrangement in great detail.

Case Study No. 4: Demonstrating Cultural Adaptability

The context is that a therapist is working with a client whose cultural upbringing is not one that the therapist is familiar with.

Application: The therapist will seek training on cultural competency and study resources that are specific to the cultural background of the client. They modify their approach to therapy so that it is more culturally sensitive, and they engage in self-reflection in order to steer clear of any possible biases.

Case Study No. 5: The Morality of an Online Presence

To provide some context, a therapist is responsible for maintaining a professional website in addition to social media presence. They share their perspectives on a variety of contentious topics in their posts.

Application: The therapist examines their internet presence and assesses whether their posts could be interpreted as being unprofessional, offensive, or in breach of ethical rules. They modify their profiles to reflect a perspective that is less biased or opinionated regarding contentious issues.

Case Study No. 6: Giving Consent After Being Informed

The context is that a therapist has lately begun using a novel therapy modality that is not considered to be part of the mainstream.

Practice Questions and Answers Explanations 2024-2025

Question 1
A therapist is practicing in California and offers teletherapy to clients in different states. Which of the following legal considerations is essential for the therapist to address?
A) Licensing reciprocity
B) Client confidentiality
C) Scope of practice
D) Informed consent

Answer 1
A) Licensing reciprocity

Explanation 1
When providing teletherapy across state lines, therapists must ensure they are in compliance with the licensing regulations of the state where the client is located. Licensing reciprocity allows therapists to practice in multiple states, provided they meet certain requirements.

Question 2
Which of the following situations would likely require a therapist to breach client confidentiality?
A) A client confesses to substance abuse
B) A client discusses their troubled marriage
C) A client expresses anger toward their boss
D) A client shares their favorite hobbies

Answer 2
A) A client confesses to substance abuse

Explanation 2
Breach of client confidentiality is warranted when a client poses a risk of harm to themselves or others, such as in the case of substance abuse.

Question 3

A therapist who is also the coach of a local soccer team begins seeing a client who is a parent of one of the team members. What should the therapist do in this situation?

A) Continue therapy and avoid mentioning the coaching role
B) Terminate therapy to avoid a dual relationship
C) Disclose the dual relationship and obtain informed consent
D) Transfer the client to another therapist

Answer 3
C) Disclose the dual relationship and obtain informed consent

Explanation 3
In situations involving a potential dual relationship, therapists should disclose the relationship, explain any potential impacts, and obtain informed consent from the client to proceed.

Question 4

In the context of therapy, what does "informed consent" refer to?

A) Providing clients with a diagnosis
B) Securing permission for video recording sessions
C) Obtaining approval for medication prescriptions
D) Gaining a client's understanding and agreement for the therapeutic process

Answer 4
D) Gaining a client's understanding and agreement for the therapeutic process

Explanation 4
Informed consent in therapy involves ensuring that clients understand the nature of therapy, its goals, potential risks, and agree to participate in the process.

Question 5

Which of the following best exemplifies a potential dual relationship for a therapist?

A) A therapist who becomes friends with a former client
B) A therapist who consults with a colleague on a case
C) A therapist who provides therapy to a family member
D) A therapist who works with a client from a different cultural background

Answer 5
A) A therapist who becomes friends with a former client

Explanation 5
Establishing a friendship with a former client can create a dual relationship, which should be approached cautiously to avoid potential ethical conflicts.

Question 6
A therapist in California has begun offering teletherapy services. What should be the primary concern when it comes to confidentiality in teletherapy?
A) Ensuring that clients have a computer with a camera
B) Using secure and encrypted communication platforms
C) Scheduling appointments at convenient times for clients
D) Recording therapy sessions for documentation purposes

Answer 6
B) Using secure and encrypted communication platforms

Explanation 6
In teletherapy, it's crucial to use secure and encrypted communication platforms to maintain client confidentiality and privacy.

Question 7
Which of the following is an example of a cultural competence approach in therapy?
A) Treating all clients the same way, regardless of their cultural background
B) Seeking ongoing education and training in cultural sensitivity
C) Avoiding clients from diverse cultural backgrounds
D) Disregarding the cultural beliefs and values of clients

Answer 7
B) Seeking ongoing education and training in cultural sensitivity

Explanation 7
Cultural competence in therapy involves continually seeking education and training to better understand and respect the cultural beliefs and values of clients from diverse backgrounds.

Question 8

A therapist is maintaining an active online presence on social media. Which of the following online behaviors should the therapist avoid to ensure ethical practice?

A) Posting personal vacation photos
B) Sharing their professional achievements
C) Offering general mental health advice
D) Engaging in respectful and educational discussions

Answer 8
A) Posting personal vacation photos

Explanation 8
Maintaining a professional online presence requires therapists to avoid sharing personal and unrelated information, such as vacation photos, to maintain ethical boundaries.

Question 9

What is the primary purpose of a treatment plan in therapy?

A) To diagnose clients accurately
B) To bill insurance companies for services
C) To outline the therapist's credentials
D) To establish goals and interventions for therapy

Answer 9
D) To establish goals and interventions for therapy

Explanation 9
A treatment plan in therapy outlines the goals, interventions, and strategies to help clients address their specific concerns and issues.

Question 10

Which of the following situations is an example of a potential boundary violation for a therapist?

A) Exchanging friendly emails with a former client
B) Celebrating a client's successful therapy outcome
C) Attending a client's social event as an invited guest
D) Offering support during a client's crisis or emergency

Answer 10

C) Attending a client's social event as an invited guest

Explanation 10
Attending a client's social event as a guest can lead to boundary violations, as it may blur the line between a professional and personal relationship.

Question 11
In therapy, what is the primary function of an assessment or diagnosis?
A) To establish long-term goals for the client
B) To create a treatment plan based on client strengths
C) To identify and understand the client's issues and needs
D) To maintain strict confidentiality of client information

Answer 11
C) To identify and understand the client's issues and needs

Explanation 11
Assessment and diagnosis in therapy help therapists identify and understand the client's specific issues and needs, which informs the treatment plan.

Question 12
A therapist is working with a client who is expressing anger toward their spouse. Which ethical principle should guide the therapist's response?
A) Autonomy
B) Non-maleficence
C) Confidentiality
D) Justice

Answer 12
A) Autonomy

Explanation 12
In this situation, respecting the client's autonomy by allowing them to express their feelings and make choices about how to address their anger is paramount.

Question 13

When conducting therapy with a minor, in addition to obtaining informed consent from the minor, who else should the therapist seek consent from?
A) The minor's teacher
B) The minor's attorney
C) The minor's parent or legal guardian
D) The minor's therapist

Answer 13
C) The minor's parent or legal guardian

Explanation 13
When working with a minor, therapists should obtain informed consent from both the minor and their parent or legal guardian.

Question 14

A therapist who is counseling a couple is facing a situation where one of the partners is unwilling to continue therapy. What ethical principle should the therapist consider?
A) Autonomy
B) Non-maleficence
C) Confidentiality
D) Veracity

Answer 14
A) Autonomy

Explanation 14
Respecting the autonomy of the individual who wishes to discontinue therapy is important. It allows clients to make their own decisions about their treatment.

Question 15

Which of the following actions by a therapist is an example of practicing cultural competence?
A) Avoiding clients from diverse cultural backgrounds
B) Treating all clients the same way, regardless of their cultural background
C) Seeking education on cultural sensitivity and adapting treatment to individual needs
D) Ignoring cultural beliefs and values when providing therapy

Answer 15
C) Seeking education on cultural sensitivity and adapting treatment to individual needs

Explanation 15
Cultural competence involves seeking education and adapting treatment to align with the unique cultural needs and values of each client.

Question 16
A therapist has a client who frequently discusses their marital issues and expresses a desire to seek a divorce. What ethical principle should the therapist be mindful of when addressing this client's concerns?
A) Autonomy
B) Non-maleficence
C) Confidentiality
D) Justice

Answer 16
A) Autonomy

Explanation 16
In this situation, respecting the client's autonomy to make choices about their marriage, including seeking a divorce, is essential.

Question 17
When conducting family therapy, what is a common ethical challenge therapists may face?
A) Protecting individual client confidentiality
B) Avoiding discussions about sensitive topics
C) Balancing the needs and privacy of multiple clients
D) Providing individual diagnosis and treatment to each family member

Answer 17
C) Balancing the needs and privacy of multiple clients

Explanation 17
In family therapy, therapists must navigate the challenge of balancing the individual needs and privacy of multiple family members while addressing the family's dynamics.

Question 18

A therapist is considering offering group therapy sessions. Which of the following should be a primary concern when establishing group therapy guidelines?

A) Ensuring complete confidentiality among group members
B) Selecting group members who have similar issues
C) Managing potential conflicts and group dynamics
D) Providing individual diagnosis and treatment to each group member

Answer 18
C) Managing potential conflicts and group dynamics

Explanation 18
Managing conflicts and group dynamics is crucial when conducting group therapy to ensure a safe and productive therapeutic environment.

Question 19

What should therapists prioritize when it comes to maintaining professional boundaries with clients?

A) Sharing personal experiences to build rapport
B) Avoiding self-disclosure
C) Exchanging gifts with clients
D) Becoming friends with clients outside of therapy

Answer 19
B) Avoiding self-disclosure

Explanation 19
Maintaining professional boundaries typically involves avoiding self-disclosure and refraining from personal relationships with clients outside of therapy.

Question 20

A therapist is considering offering a sliding fee scale to accommodate clients with lower income. What ethical principle does this align with?

A) Non-maleficence
B) Beneficence
C) Autonomy
D) Justice

Answer 20
D) Justice

Explanation 20
Offering a sliding fee scale is an ethical practice that aligns with the principle of justice, ensuring that therapy services are accessible to individuals with varying financial means.

Question 21
A client's partner, who is also the therapist's friend, calls the therapist to discuss the client's therapy progress. What should the therapist do in this situation?
A) Provide the partner with information about the client's therapy
B) Maintain confidentiality and refrain from discussing the client's progress
C) Advise the partner to attend a joint therapy session with the client
D) Encourage the partner to contact the client directly

Answer 21
B) Maintain confidentiality and refrain from discussing the client's progress

Explanation 21
Maintaining the confidentiality of the client and not discussing their progress with the therapist's friend is the ethical course of action.

Question 22
A therapist is faced with a situation where a client is threatening harm to themselves. What ethical principle should guide the therapist's actions?
A) Autonomy
B) Non-maleficence
C) Veracity
D) Beneficence

Answer 22
B) Non-maleficence

Explanation 22
In this situation, the ethical principle of non-maleficence requires the therapist to take action to prevent harm to the client, even if it means breaching confidentiality.

Question 23

A therapist is working with a client who belongs to a culture with very different beliefs and values. What is the therapist's primary responsibility in this situation?

A) Change the client's beliefs to align with the therapist's values

B) Respect and adapt to the client's cultural beliefs and values

C) Refer the client to a therapist from their own cultural background

D) Avoid discussing cultural beliefs to prevent potential conflicts

Answer 23

B) Respect and adapt to the client's cultural beliefs and values

Explanation 23

The therapist's primary responsibility is to respect and adapt to the client's cultural beliefs and values to provide culturally sensitive care.

Question 24

A therapist is considering joining a support group for mental health professionals to discuss their work experiences. Which ethical principle should the therapist consider when participating in such a group?

A) Confidentiality

B) Autonomy

C) Beneficence

D) Veracity

Answer 24

A) Confidentiality

Explanation 24

Participating in a support group for mental health professionals requires a commitment to maintaining client confidentiality and respecting the privacy of client-related discussions.

Question 25

A therapist working with a couple begins to experience strong personal biases against one of the partners. What should the therapist do to address this situation ethically?

A) Continue therapy while concealing personal biases

B) Terminate therapy with the couple

C) Seek supervision or consultation to address their biases

D) Encourage the partner to seek therapy elsewhere

Answer 25
C) Seek supervision or consultation to address their biases

Explanation 25
Seeking supervision or consultation is a responsible ethical approach when a therapist is dealing with personal biases that could affect their objectivity and fairness in therapy.

Question 26
When providing therapy to a minor, what should a therapist typically do in terms of informed consent?
A) Obtain informed consent from the minor only
B) Obtain informed consent from the minor's parent or legal guardian only
C) Not worry about informed consent, as it is not applicable to minors
D) Obtain informed consent from both the minor and their parent or legal guardian

Answer 26
D) Obtain informed consent from both the minor and their parent or legal guardian

Explanation 26
When providing therapy to a minor, it is typically necessary to obtain informed consent from both the minor and their parent or legal guardian to ensure transparency and legal compliance.

Question 27
In the context of therapy, what does the principle of "non-maleficence" emphasize?
A) Respecting client autonomy
B) Avoiding harm to clients
C) Benefiting clients
D) Respecting client confidentiality

Answer 27
B) Avoiding harm to clients

Explanation 27

The principle of non-maleficence focuses on the therapist's duty to avoid causing harm to their clients.

Question 28
A therapist receives a gift from a client as a gesture of appreciation. What ethical principle should guide the therapist's response to this situation?
A) Autonomy
B) Non-maleficence
C) Beneficence
D) Professional boundaries

Answer 28
D) Professional boundaries

Explanation 28
Receiving gifts from clients can pose ethical dilemmas. The therapist should consider the impact on professional boundaries and ethical guidelines.

Question 29
A therapist is working with a client who is struggling with substance abuse. The client confesses to illegal drug use. What ethical principle should guide the therapist's actions in this situation?
A) Autonomy
B) Veracity
C) Beneficence
D) Professional boundaries

Answer 29
B) Veracity

Explanation 29
The ethical principle of veracity requires the therapist to be truthful and honest in their interactions. In this case, it may involve addressing the illegal drug use with the client.

Question 30
What is the primary purpose of a professional code of ethics for Marriage and Family Therapists?
A) To outline billing procedures
B) To specify the therapist's credentials

C) To provide guidelines for ethical practice
D) To describe therapeutic techniques

Answer 30
C) To provide guidelines for ethical practice

Explanation 30
A professional code of ethics for Marriage and Family Therapists serves as a set of guidelines for ethical practice and conduct.

Question 31
A therapist is seeking consultation with a colleague to discuss a particularly challenging case. What ethical principle is the therapist demonstrating?
A) Autonomy
B) Non-maleficence
C) Veracity
D) Beneficence

Answer 31
D) Beneficence

Explanation 31
Seeking consultation with a colleague to ensure the best possible care for the client demonstrates the ethical principle of beneficence.

Question 32
A therapist is working with a client who has a history of self-harm. What should the therapist prioritize in this situation?
A) Beneficence
B) Autonomy
C) Non-maleficence
D) Veracity

Answer 32
C) Non-maleficence

Explanation 32
Non-maleficence is the ethical principle that emphasizes the therapist's duty to avoid harm. When working with a client who has a history of self-harm, preventing harm is a top priority.

Question 33

What is the primary goal of obtaining informed consent from clients in therapy?
A) To confirm the therapist's qualifications
B) To secure the client's agreement to pay for services
C) To ensure that the therapist has liability insurance
D) To ensure that clients understand the nature of therapy and agree to participate

Answer 33

D) To ensure that clients understand the nature of therapy and agree to participate

Explanation 33

Obtaining informed consent in therapy is primarily about ensuring that clients fully understand the therapeutic process and agree to participate.

Question 34

In therapy, what is the primary function of assessment and diagnosis?
A) To establish rapport with clients
B) To provide legal testimony if needed
C) To identify and understand the client's issues and needs
D) To offer a diagnosis for insurance billing purposes

Answer 34

C) To identify and understand the client's issues and needs

Explanation 34

Assessment and diagnosis in therapy aim to identify and understand the client's specific issues and needs, which inform the treatment plan.

Question 35

A therapist is working with a client from a different cultural background. What should be the therapist's primary approach to ensure effective therapy?
A) Attempt to change the client's cultural beliefs
B) Avoid discussing cultural beliefs and values
C) Respect and adapt to the client's cultural beliefs and values
D) Refer the client to another therapist from their cultural background

Answer 35
C) Respect and adapt to the client's cultural beliefs and values

Explanation 35
To provide effective therapy to a client from a different cultural background, therapists should respect and adapt to the client's cultural beliefs and values.

Question 36
A therapist is working with a client who expresses a desire to discontinue therapy. What ethical principle should guide the therapist's response?
A) Non-maleficence
B) Autonomy
C) Beneficence
D) Professional boundaries

Answer 36
B) Autonomy

Explanation 36
When a client wishes to discontinue therapy, respecting their autonomy and choice is the ethical course of action.

Question 37
What is a common ethical challenge therapists may face when providing therapy to minors?
A) Respecting client autonomy
B) Balancing the needs and privacy of multiple clients
C) Obtaining informed consent from minors
D) Providing a diagnosis for insurance billing

Answer 37
B) Balancing the needs and privacy of multiple clients

Explanation 37
Providing therapy to minors often involves balancing the needs and privacy of both the minor and their parent or legal guardian, presenting an ethical challenge.

Question 38

A therapist is working with a family in therapy. What ethical principle is crucial when addressing issues related to family dynamics and privacy?
A) Autonomy
B) Non-maleficence
C) Beneficence
D) Confidentiality

Answer 38
D) Confidentiality

Explanation 38
When working with a family in therapy, maintaining confidentiality while addressing family dynamics and privacy is a critical ethical consideration.

Question 39

A therapist is considering offering group therapy sessions. What ethical principle should guide the therapist's selection of group members?
A) Non-maleficence
B) Respecting client autonomy
C) Balancing the needs and privacy of multiple clients
D) Professional boundaries

Answer 39
C) Balancing the needs and privacy of multiple clients

Explanation 39
When selecting group members for group therapy, therapists must consider the balance of individual client needs and privacy, which aligns with the ethical principle of maintaining professional boundaries.

Question 40

A therapist is working with a client who has expressed a romantic interest in the therapist. What ethical principle should guide the therapist's response to this situation?
A) Non-maleficence
B) Autonomy
C) Beneficence
D) Professional boundaries

Answer 40
D) Professional boundaries

Explanation 40
Maintaining professional boundaries is essential when a client expresses a romantic interest in the therapist. Ethical guidelines advise therapists to address this situation with clear boundaries and professionalism.

Question 41
A therapist is working with a couple who frequently argues during therapy sessions. What ethical principle should guide the therapist's approach to managing conflicts within the therapy setting?
A) Non-maleficence
B) Confidentiality
C) Beneficence
D) Maintaining professional boundaries

Answer 41
A) Non-maleficence

Explanation 41
The therapist's primary ethical duty in managing conflicts within the therapy setting is to avoid causing harm to clients, aligning with the principle of non-maleficence.

Question 42
When providing therapy to a family, what should therapists prioritize in terms of informed consent?
A) Obtaining informed consent from the family as a whole
B) Ensuring that all family members agree with the therapist's approach
C) Obtaining informed consent from individual family members
D) Not worrying about informed consent within a family context

Answer 42
C) Obtaining informed consent from individual family members

Explanation 42
In family therapy, therapists should prioritize obtaining informed consent from individual family members, as they are separate clients with unique needs and privacy considerations.

Question 43

A therapist is working with a client who has a history of trauma and shares traumatic experiences during therapy. What ethical principle should guide the therapist's approach in this situation?

A) Autonomy
B) Non-maleficence
C) Beneficence
D) Professional boundaries

Answer 43
B) Non-maleficence

Explanation 43
The ethical principle of non-maleficence is essential when working with clients who have a history of trauma, as the therapist must avoid retraumatizing the client.

Question 44

A therapist is considering offering reduced-fee therapy services for clients with financial constraints. What ethical principle does this align with?

A) Autonomy
B) Beneficence
C) Non-maleficence
D) Professional boundaries

Answer 44
B) Beneficence

Explanation 44
Offering reduced-fee therapy services for clients with financial constraints is an ethical practice that aligns with the principle of beneficence, which emphasizes doing good and providing help to clients.

Question 45

A therapist is working with a client who has recently experienced the loss of a loved one. What ethical principle should guide the therapist's response to this client's grief?

A) Autonomy
B) Non-maleficence

C) Beneficence
D) Professional boundaries

Answer 45
C) Beneficence

Explanation 45
In this situation, the therapist's ethical duty is to provide support and assistance to the grieving client, aligning with the principle of beneficence.

Question 46
A therapist is working with a client who is considering a major life decision. What ethical principle should guide the therapist's approach to supporting the client's decision-making process?
A) Non-maleficence
B) Autonomy
C) Beneficence
D) Professional boundaries

Answer 46
B) Autonomy

Explanation 46
When clients are making significant life decisions, therapists should respect their autonomy and support their capacity to make choices.

Question 47
A therapist is seeking supervision to discuss a challenging case and receive guidance from a more experienced colleague. What ethical principle is the therapist demonstrating?
A) Non-maleficence
B) Autonomy
C) Beneficence
D) Veracity

Answer 47
C) Beneficence

Explanation 47

Seeking supervision for guidance in a challenging case demonstrates the therapist's commitment to the ethical principle of beneficence, which is about promoting the well-being of the client.

Question 48
A therapist is working with a client who has experienced a traumatic event. What should be the therapist's primary goal in this therapeutic context?
A) To ensure the client is comfortable and at ease
B) To obtain informed consent from the client's family
C) To avoid discussing the traumatic event
D) To create a safe and supportive environment for processing the trauma

Answer 48
D) To create a safe and supportive environment for processing the trauma

Explanation 48
When working with clients who have experienced trauma, the therapist's primary goal should be to create a safe and supportive environment to help the client process the trauma.

Question 49
A therapist is working with a couple who frequently argues during therapy sessions. What ethical principle should guide the therapist's approach to managing conflicts within the therapy setting?
A) Beneficence
B) Confidentiality
C) Non-maleficence
D) Autonomy

Answer 49
C) Non-maleficence

Explanation 49
When conflicts arise during therapy sessions, the therapist should prioritize the ethical principle of non-maleficence by avoiding harm to the clients and ensuring their safety.

Question 50
A therapist is working with a client who has expressed strong religious beliefs. What ethical principle should guide the therapist's approach to respecting the client's beliefs?
A) Autonomy
B) Non-maleficence
C) Beneficence
D) Professional boundaries

Answer 50
A) Autonomy

Explanation 50
In working with a client with strong religious beliefs, respecting their autonomy and choices related to their beliefs is an ethical consideration.

Question 51
A therapist is working with a client who has a history of self-harm and currently exhibits self-destructive behavior. What ethical principle should guide the therapist's actions?
A) Autonomy
B) Non-maleficence
C) Beneficence
D) Professional boundaries

Answer 51
B) Non-maleficence

Explanation 51
The therapist's primary ethical duty in this situation is to prevent harm to the client, which aligns with the principle of non-maleficence.

Question 52
A therapist is working with a client who is experiencing significant distress and has disclosed thoughts of self-harm. What ethical principle should guide the therapist's actions in this situation?
A) Non-maleficence
B) Autonomy
C) Beneficence

D) Veracity

Answer 52
A) Non-maleficence

Explanation 52
In this situation, the therapist's primary ethical duty is to prevent harm to the client, which aligns with the principle of non-maleficence.

Question 53
What should a therapist prioritize when working with clients from diverse cultural backgrounds?
A) Imposing their own cultural beliefs on clients
B) Avoiding discussions about cultural differences
C) Respecting and adapting to clients' cultural beliefs and values
D) Refusing to provide therapy to clients from diverse backgrounds

Answer 53
C) Respecting and adapting to clients' cultural beliefs and values

Explanation 53
When working with clients from diverse cultural backgrounds, therapists should prioritize respecting and adapting to the clients' cultural beliefs and values to provide culturally sensitive care.

Question 54
A therapist is considering offering teletherapy services. What ethical principle should guide the therapist's actions to ensure client confidentiality during online sessions?
A) Non-maleficence
B) Beneficence
C) Autonomy
D) Veracity

Answer 54
A) Non-maleficence

Explanation 54

To ensure client confidentiality during teletherapy, therapists should prioritize the ethical principle of non-maleficence by taking steps to avoid harm to the client's privacy.

Question 55

A therapist is faced with a situation where a client discloses a desire to harm someone else. What ethical principle should guide the therapist's actions?
A) Autonomy
B) Beneficence
C) Non-maleficence
D) Professional boundaries

Answer 55
B) Beneficence

Explanation 55
In this situation, the therapist's ethical duty is to protect potential victims and ensure the well-being of others, which aligns with the principle of beneficence.

Question 56

A therapist is considering using play therapy techniques with a child client. What ethical principle should guide the therapist's choice of therapeutic approach?
A) Non-maleficence
B) Autonomy
C) Beneficence
D) Professional boundaries

Answer 56
C) Beneficence

Explanation 56
The therapist's choice to use play therapy techniques with a child client should align with the principle of beneficence, which aims to promote the well-being and development of the child.

Question 57

A therapist is working with a client who has experienced severe trauma. What should be the therapist's primary concern when using trauma-focused interventions?
A) Ensuring the client is comfortable and relaxed
B) Avoiding any discussion of the traumatic experiences
C) Creating a safe and supportive environment for trauma processing
D) Maintaining professional boundaries

Answer 57
C) Creating a safe and supportive environment for trauma processing

Explanation 57
When using trauma-focused interventions, the therapist's primary concern should be to create a safe and supportive environment for the client to process their trauma.

Question 58

A therapist is considering offering family therapy sessions. What ethical principle should guide the therapist's approach to balancing the needs and privacy of multiple family members?
A) Autonomy
B) Non-maleficence
C) Beneficence
D) Confidentiality

Answer 58
D) Confidentiality

Explanation 58
Balancing the needs and privacy of multiple family members while providing family therapy involves respecting individual confidentiality, which aligns with the principle of confidentiality.

Question 59

A therapist is working with a client who has expressed concerns about their family's well-being. What ethical principle should guide the therapist's approach to addressing these concerns?
A) Beneficence
B) Non-maleficence

C) Professional boundaries
D) Veracity

Answer 59
A) Beneficence

Explanation 59
Addressing a client's concerns about their family's well-being aligns with the ethical principle of beneficence, which focuses on promoting the well-being and best interests of the client.

Question 60
A therapist is considering offering art therapy as a therapeutic approach. What ethical principle should guide the therapist's choice of therapeutic techniques?
A) Non-maleficence
B) Autonomy
C) Beneficence
D) Professional boundaries

Answer 60
A) Non-maleficence

Explanation 60
When considering therapeutic techniques like art therapy, therapists should prioritize the ethical principle of non-maleficence by ensuring that the techniques do not cause harm to the client.

Question 61
A therapist is working with a client who is hesitant to discuss their traumatic experiences. What ethical principle should guide the therapist's approach to supporting the client through this process?
A) Autonomy
B) Beneficence
C) Non-maleficence
D) Veracity

Answer 61
A) Autonomy

Explanation 61

Respecting the client's autonomy and choice in discussing traumatic experiences is an ethical consideration in this situation.

Question 62

A therapist is working with a client who has expressed a desire to terminate therapy. What ethical principle should guide the therapist's response?
A) Non-maleficence
B) Beneficence
C) Autonomy
D) Veracity

Answer 62
C) Autonomy

Explanation 62
When a client wishes to terminate therapy, respecting their autonomy and choice is the ethical course of action.

Question 63

A therapist is working with a client who has a history of substance abuse. What should be the therapist's primary concern in this therapeutic context?
A) Beneficence
B) Autonomy
C) Non-maleficence
D) Professional boundaries

Answer 63
C) Non-maleficence

Explanation 63
Working with a client who has a history of substance abuse, the therapist's primary concern is to prevent harm and avoid exacerbating the client's issues, which aligns with the principle of non-maleficence.

Question 64

A therapist is working with a client who is considering ending their long-term marriage. What ethical principle should guide the therapist's approach to supporting the client's decision?
A) Autonomy
B) Beneficence

C) Non-maleficence
D) Veracity

Answer 64
A) Autonomy

Explanation 64
Supporting a client's decision regarding their long-term marriage should be guided by the principle of autonomy, respecting their ability to make choices about their own life.

Question 65
A therapist is working with a client who is experiencing significant distress and has difficulty expressing their emotions verbally. What ethical principle should guide the therapist's choice of therapeutic techniques?
A) Non-maleficence
B) Beneficence
C) Autonomy
D) Professional boundaries

Answer 65
B) Beneficence

Explanation 65
Selecting therapeutic techniques that help the client express their emotions aligns with the principle of beneficence, as it promotes the client's emotional well-being and development.

Question 66
A therapist is working with a client who has a history of depression and suicidal thoughts. What should be the therapist's primary concern in this therapeutic context?
A) Autonomy
B) Non-maleficence
C) Beneficence
D) Professional boundaries

Answer 66
B) Non-maleficence

Explanation 66
Working with a client who has a history of depression and suicidal thoughts, the therapist's primary concern is to prevent harm to the client, which aligns with the principle of non-maleficence.

Question 67
A therapist is working with a client who is experiencing severe anxiety. What ethical principle should guide the therapist's approach to treatment?
A) Beneficence
B) Autonomy
C) Non-maleficence
D) Professional boundaries

Answer 67
A) Beneficence

Explanation 67
The therapist's primary goal when working with a client experiencing severe anxiety is to promote their well-being and alleviate distress, aligning with the principle of beneficence.

Question 68
A therapist is considering using cognitive-behavioral therapy (CBT) techniques with a client. What ethical principle should guide the therapist's choice of therapeutic approach?
A) Non-maleficence
B) Autonomy
C) Beneficence
D) Professional boundaries

Answer 68
C) Beneficence

Explanation 68
The therapist's choice to use CBT techniques should align with the principle of beneficence, aiming to promote the client's well-being and mental health.

Question 69

A therapist is working with a client who has been recently diagnosed with a serious medical condition. What ethical principle should guide the therapist's approach to supporting the client through this difficult time?
A) Autonomy
B) Non-maleficence
C) Beneficence
D) Veracity

Answer 69
C) Beneficence

Explanation 69
Supporting a client who has been diagnosed with a serious medical condition should be guided by the principle of beneficence, aiming to promote the client's well-being and provide emotional support.

Question 70

A therapist is working with a client who is a minor and has disclosed experiencing abuse at home. What ethical principle should guide the therapist's actions in this situation?
A) Beneficence
B) Autonomy
C) Non-maleficence
D) Veracity

Answer 70
A) Beneficence

Explanation 70
In situations where a minor client discloses abuse, the therapist's primary ethical concern is the well-being and safety of the client, aligning with the principle of beneficence.

Question 71

A therapist is considering providing therapy to a client who has a history of legal issues. What ethical principle should guide the therapist's approach to therapy in this context?
A) Autonomy
B) Beneficence

C) Non-maleficence
D) Professional boundaries

Answer 71
D) Professional boundaries

Explanation 71
When working with a client who has a history of legal issues, therapists should establish and maintain clear professional boundaries to ensure ethical practice.

Question 72
A therapist is working with a client who is experiencing grief and loss. What ethical principle should guide the therapist's approach to supporting the client through the grieving process?
A) Beneficence
B) Autonomy
C) Non-maleficence
D) Professional boundaries

Answer 72
A) Beneficence

Explanation 72
Supporting a client experiencing grief and loss is guided by the principle of beneficence, which focuses on promoting their emotional well-being and coping.

Question 73
A therapist is working with a client who is hesitant to share their sexual orientation due to fear of judgment. What ethical principle should guide the therapist's approach to creating a safe and supportive environment for the client?
A) Autonomy
B) Non-maleficence
C) Beneficence
D) Professional boundaries

Answer 73
C) Beneficence

Explanation 73
Creating a safe and supportive environment for a client who is hesitant to share their sexual orientation aligns with the principle of beneficence, promoting their emotional well-being and comfort.

Question 74
A therapist is considering offering family therapy services. What ethical principle should guide the therapist's approach to protecting the privacy of family members during sessions?
A) Autonomy
B) Non-maleficence
C) Confidentiality
D) Professional boundaries

Answer 74
C) Confidentiality

Explanation 74
Maintaining the confidentiality of family members during family therapy sessions is an ethical consideration guided by the principle of confidentiality.

Question 75
A therapist is working with a client who has experienced a recent trauma. What ethical principle should guide the therapist's approach to addressing the trauma?
A) Beneficence
B) Autonomy
C) Non-maleficence
D) Veracity

Answer 75
A) Beneficence

Explanation 75
Supporting a client who has experienced a recent trauma aligns with the principle of beneficence, focusing on promoting the client's well-being and coping.

Question 76

A therapist is considering using narrative therapy techniques with a client. What ethical principle should guide the therapist's choice of therapeutic approach?
A) Non-maleficence
B) Autonomy
C) Beneficence
D) Professional boundaries

Answer 76
B) Autonomy

Explanation 76
The therapist's choice to use narrative therapy techniques should align with the principle of autonomy, allowing the client to shape their own therapeutic narrative.

Question 77

A therapist is working with a client who is struggling with gender identity. What ethical principle should guide the therapist's approach to supporting the client's exploration of their identity?
A) Non-maleficence
B) Beneficence
C) Autonomy
D) Professional boundaries

Answer 77
C) Autonomy

Explanation 77
Supporting a client's exploration of their gender identity should be guided by the principle of autonomy, respecting the client's choices and self-discovery.

Question 78

A therapist is considering offering online therapy services. What ethical principle should guide the therapist's actions to ensure the security and privacy of online therapy sessions?
A) Non-maleficence
B) Beneficence
C) Autonomy

D) Veracity

Answer 78
A) Non-maleficence

Explanation 78
Ensuring the security and privacy of online therapy sessions is guided by the ethical principle of non-maleficence, which aims to prevent harm to the client's privacy.

Question 79
A therapist is working with a client who is experiencing distress related to a recent breakup. What ethical principle should guide the therapist's approach to providing support and counseling?
A) Beneficence
B) Autonomy
C) Non-maleficence
D) Professional boundaries

Answer 79
A) Beneficence

Explanation 79
Providing support and counseling to a client going through a breakup is guided by the principle of beneficence, focusing on promoting the client's emotional well-being.

Question 80
A therapist is considering using art therapy techniques with a client. What ethical principle should guide the therapist's choice of therapeutic approach?
A) Non-maleficence
B) Autonomy
C) Beneficence
D) Professional boundaries

Answer 80
C) Beneficence

Explanation 80

The therapist's choice to use art therapy techniques should align with the principle of beneficence, promoting the client's emotional well-being and self-expression.

Question 81

A therapist is working with a client who is reluctant to share certain personal details. What ethical principle should guide the therapist's approach to respecting the client's boundaries?
A) Beneficence
B) Autonomy
C) Non-maleficence
D) Professional boundaries

Answer 81
B) Autonomy

Explanation 81
Respecting a client's reluctance to share certain personal details aligns with the ethical principle of autonomy, allowing the client to set their boundaries.

Question 82

A therapist is working with a client who has a history of self-harm. What ethical principle should guide the therapist's approach to assessing and managing self-harming behavior?
A) Beneficence
B) Non-maleficence
C) Autonomy
D) Professional boundaries

Answer 82
B) Non-maleficence

Explanation 82
When dealing with a client who has a history of self-harm, the therapist's primary ethical duty is to prevent harm to the client, which aligns with the principle of non-maleficence.

Question 83

A therapist is working with a couple who frequently argues during therapy sessions. What ethical principle should guide the therapist's approach to managing conflicts within the therapy setting?
A) Beneficence
B) Autonomy
C) Non-maleficence
D) Professional boundaries

Answer 83
C) Non-maleficence

Explanation 83
The therapist should prioritize the ethical principle of non-maleficence by avoiding harm to the clients when managing conflicts within therapy sessions.

Question 84

A therapist is working with a client who has been diagnosed with a severe mental illness. What ethical principle should guide the therapist's approach to treatment?
A) Autonomy
B) Beneficence
C) Non-maleficence
D) Professional boundaries

Answer 84
B) Beneficence

Explanation 84
The therapist's ethical duty when working with a client diagnosed with a severe mental illness is to promote the client's well-being, aligning with the principle of beneficence.

Question 85

A therapist is considering using play therapy techniques with a child client. What ethical principle should guide the therapist's choice of therapeutic approach?
A) Non-maleficence
B) Autonomy
C) Beneficence

D) Professional boundaries

Answer 85
C) Beneficence

Explanation 85
The therapist's choice to use play therapy techniques with a child client should align with the principle of beneficence, which promotes the child's emotional well-being and development.

Question 86
A therapist is working with a client who has experienced trauma and is struggling with intrusive memories. What ethical principle should guide the therapist's approach to addressing these intrusive memories?
A) Autonomy
B) Beneficence
C) Non-maleficence
D) Professional boundaries

Answer 86
C) Non-maleficence

Explanation 86
The therapist's primary ethical duty when working with a client struggling with intrusive memories is to prevent harm and avoid retraumatization, which aligns with the principle of non-maleficence.

Question 87
A therapist is considering providing therapy to a family. What ethical principle should guide the therapist's approach to balancing the needs and privacy of multiple family members?
A) Autonomy
B) Non-maleficence
C) Confidentiality
D) Professional boundaries

Answer 87
C) Confidentiality

Explanation 87

Balancing the needs and privacy of multiple family members in family therapy involves maintaining individual confidentiality, guided by the principle of confidentiality.

Question 88
A therapist is working with a client who has been a victim of domestic violence. What ethical principle should guide the therapist's approach to ensuring the client's safety?
A) Beneficence
B) Autonomy
C) Non-maleficence
D) Professional boundaries

Answer 88
A) Beneficence

Explanation 88
Ensuring the safety of a client who has been a victim of domestic violence is guided by the ethical principle of beneficence, which focuses on promoting the client's well-being.

Question 89
A therapist is working with a client who is struggling with depression and has a history of suicidal thoughts. What ethical principle should guide the therapist's approach to providing support and intervention?
A) Autonomy
B) Beneficence
C) Non-maleficence
D) Professional boundaries

Answer 89
B) Beneficence

Explanation 89
Providing support and intervention to a client struggling with depression and suicidal thoughts is guided by the principle of beneficence, aiming to promote the client's well-being and safety.

Question 90

A therapist is working with a couple, and one partner has a history of infidelity. What ethical principle should guide the therapist's approach to addressing trust and fidelity issues within the relationship?

A) Autonomy

B) Non-maleficence

C) Beneficence

D) Professional boundaries

Answer 90

C) Beneficence

Explanation 90

The therapist's ethical duty in addressing trust and fidelity issues in the relationship is to promote the well-being and healing of the couple, aligning with the principle of beneficence.

Question 91

A therapist is considering using mindfulness-based therapy techniques with a client. What ethical principle should guide the therapist's choice of therapeutic approach?

A) Autonomy

B) Non-maleficence

C) Beneficence

D) Professional boundaries

Answer 91

C) Beneficence

Explanation 91

The therapist's choice to use mindfulness-based therapy techniques should align with the principle of beneficence, which promotes the client's emotional well-being and self-awareness.

Question 92

A therapist is working with a client who is hesitant to disclose a recent crime they committed. What ethical principle should guide the therapist's approach to addressing this issue?

A) Autonomy

B) Non-maleficence

C) Beneficence
D) Professional boundaries

Answer 92
A) Autonomy

Explanation 92
Respecting the client's autonomy and choice to disclose a recent crime is an ethical consideration in this situation.

Question 93
A therapist is considering using family systems therapy techniques with a client. What ethical principle should guide the therapist's choice of therapeutic approach?
A) Non-maleficence
B) Beneficence
C) Autonomy
D) Professional boundaries

Answer 93
C) Autonomy

Explanation 93
The therapist's choice to use family systems therapy techniques should align with the principle of autonomy, allowing the client to shape their therapeutic process.

Question 94
A therapist is working with a client who is a minor and is considering an abortion. What ethical principle should guide the therapist's approach to supporting the client's decision?
A) Beneficence
B) Autonomy
C) Non-maleficence
D) Professional boundaries

Answer 94
B) Autonomy

Explanation 94

Supporting a minor client's decision regarding an abortion should be guided by the principle of autonomy, respecting their ability to make choices about their own body.

Question 95

A therapist is working with a client who is hesitant to share their gender identity due to fear of discrimination. What ethical principle should guide the therapist's approach to creating a safe and supportive environment for the client?

A) Beneficence
B) Autonomy
C) Non-maleficence
D) Professional boundaries

Answer 95
A) Beneficence

Explanation 95
Creating a safe and supportive environment for a client who is hesitant to share their gender identity aligns with the principle of beneficence, promoting their emotional well-being and comfort.

Question 96

A therapist is working with a client who has a history of substance abuse. What ethical principle should guide the therapist's approach to addressing the client's addiction issues?

A) Autonomy
B) Beneficence
C) Non-maleficence
D) Professional boundaries

Answer 96
B) Beneficence

Explanation 96
Addressing a client's addiction issues is guided by the principle of beneficence, aiming to promote the client's well-being and recovery.

Question 97

A therapist is working with a family in therapy. What ethical principle should guide the therapist's approach to ensuring the best interests of the children within the family?
A) Non-maleficence
B) Beneficence
C) Autonomy
D) Professional boundaries

Answer 97
B) Beneficence

Explanation 97
The therapist's ethical duty when working with a family is to ensure the best interests of the children, aligning with the principle of beneficence.

Question 98

A therapist is considering offering online therapy services. What ethical principle should guide the therapist's actions to ensure the informed consent of clients receiving online therapy?
A) Autonomy
B) Beneficence
C) Non-maleficence
D) Veracity

Answer 98
A) Autonomy

Explanation 98
Ensuring the informed consent of clients receiving online therapy is guided by the principle of autonomy, respecting their ability to make choices regarding their treatment.

Question 99

A therapist is working with a client who has been recently diagnosed with a terminal illness. What ethical principle should guide the therapist's approach to providing support and counseling during this challenging time?
A) Beneficence
B) Autonomy
C) Non-maleficence

D) Professional boundaries

Answer 99
A) Beneficence

Explanation 99
Supporting a client who has been diagnosed with a terminal illness is guided by the principle of beneficence, aiming to promote the client's emotional well-being and coping.

Question 100
A therapist is working with a client who is a minor and is experiencing significant distress due to parental conflict. What ethical principle should guide the therapist's approach to helping the client cope with the situation?
A) Autonomy
B) Beneficence
C) Non-maleficence
D) Professional boundaries

Answer 100
B) Beneficence

Explanation 100
Helping a minor client cope with significant distress due to parental conflict is guided by the principle of beneficence, focusing on promoting the client's well-being and emotional stability.

Question 101
A therapist is working with a client who has been involved in a recent legal dispute. What ethical principle should guide the therapist's approach to addressing the client's legal concerns?
A) Non-maleficence
B) Autonomy
C) Beneficence
D) Professional boundaries

Answer 101
D) Professional boundaries

Explanation 101

When addressing a client's legal concerns, therapists should establish and maintain clear professional boundaries to ensure ethical practice.

Question 102
A therapist is considering using art therapy techniques with a client. What ethical principle should guide the therapist's choice of therapeutic approach?
A) Beneficence
B) Autonomy
C) Non-maleficence
D) Professional boundaries

Answer 102
C) Non-maleficence

Explanation 102
The therapist's choice to use art therapy techniques should align with the principle of non-maleficence, ensuring that the techniques do not cause harm to the client.

Question 103
A therapist is working with a client who has been a victim of sexual assault. What ethical principle should guide the therapist's approach to providing trauma-focused therapy?
A) Autonomy
B) Beneficence
C) Non-maleficence
D) Professional boundaries

Answer 103
B) Beneficence

Explanation 103
Providing trauma-focused therapy to a client who has been a victim of sexual assault is guided by the principle of beneficence, aiming to promote the client's well-being and healing.

Question 104

A therapist is working with a client who is hesitant to discuss their past abusive relationship. What ethical principle should guide the therapist's approach to supporting the client through this process?

A) Non-maleficence
B) Autonomy
C) Beneficence
D) Professional boundaries

Answer 104
B) Autonomy

Explanation 104
Respecting the client's autonomy and choice in discussing their past abusive relationship is an ethical consideration in this situation.

Question 105

A therapist is working with a client who is reluctant to participate in couples therapy. What ethical principle should guide the therapist's approach to respecting the client's autonomy in the therapeutic process?

A) Beneficence
B) Non-maleficence
C) Autonomy
D) Professional boundaries

Answer 105
C) Autonomy

Explanation 105
Respecting the client's autonomy and choice to participate in couples therapy is guided by the principle of autonomy.

Question 106

A therapist is working with a client who is struggling with eating disorders. What ethical principle should guide the therapist's approach to addressing these issues?

A) Non-maleficence
B) Beneficence
C) Autonomy
D) Professional boundaries

Answer 106
B) Beneficence

Explanation 106
Addressing a client's eating disorders is guided by the principle of beneficence, focusing on promoting the client's well-being and recovery.

Question 107
A therapist is considering offering group therapy services. What ethical principle should guide the therapist's approach to maintaining the privacy and confidentiality of group members?
A) Autonomy
B) Non-maleficence
C) Confidentiality
D) Professional boundaries

Answer 107
C) Confidentiality

Explanation 107
Maintaining the privacy and confidentiality of group members in group therapy involves respecting individual confidentiality, which aligns with the principle of confidentiality.

Question 108
A therapist is working with a client who is struggling with issues related to their sexual orientation. What ethical principle should guide the therapist's approach to providing affirmative therapy for LGBTQ+ clients?
A) Beneficence
B) Autonomy
C) Non-maleficence
D) Professional boundaries

Answer 108
A) Beneficence

Explanation 108
Providing affirmative therapy for LGBTQ+ clients is guided by the principle of beneficence, aiming to promote the well-being and mental health of the client.

Question 109

A therapist is considering offering online therapy services. What ethical principle should guide the therapist's actions to ensure the competence of online therapy practice?

A) Autonomy
B) Beneficence
C) Non-maleficence
D) Professional boundaries

Answer 109
B) Beneficence

Explanation 109
Ensuring the competence of online therapy practice is guided by the ethical principle of beneficence, aiming to provide high-quality and effective treatment to clients.

Question 110

A therapist is working with a couple who is experiencing fertility issues and is considering fertility treatments. What ethical principle should guide the therapist's approach to supporting the couple's decision?

A) Autonomy
B) Non-maleficence
C) Beneficence
D) Professional boundaries

Answer 110
A) Autonomy

Explanation 110
Supporting the couple's decision regarding fertility treatments should be guided by the principle of autonomy, respecting their ability to make choices about their reproductive health.

Question 111

A therapist is working with a client who has been diagnosed with a severe personality disorder. What ethical principle should guide the therapist's approach to treatment and support?
A) Beneficence
B) Autonomy
C) Non-maleficence
D) Professional boundaries

Answer 111
A) Beneficence

Explanation 111
The therapist's ethical duty when working with a client diagnosed with a severe personality disorder is to promote the client's well-being and provide effective support, aligning with the principle of beneficence.

Question 112

A therapist is working with a family in therapy, and there are cultural differences among family members. What ethical principle should guide the therapist's approach to respecting and adapting to cultural beliefs and values?
A) Beneficence
B) Autonomy
C) Non-maleficence
D) Professional boundaries

Answer 112
B) Autonomy

Explanation 112
Respecting and adapting to cultural beliefs and values within a family therapy context aligns with the ethical principle of autonomy, allowing clients to maintain their cultural identity and preferences.

Question 113

A therapist is considering using cognitive-behavioral therapy (CBT) techniques with a client. What ethical principle should guide the therapist's choice of therapeutic approach?
A) Non-maleficence
B) Autonomy

C) Beneficence
D) Professional boundaries

Answer 113
C) Beneficence

Explanation 113
The therapist's choice to use CBT techniques should align with the principle of beneficence, aiming to promote the client's well-being and mental health.

Question 114
A therapist is working with a client who is a minor and has disclosed experiencing bullying at school. What ethical principle should guide the therapist's actions in this situation?
A) Autonomy
B) Non-maleficence
C) Beneficence
D) Veracity

Answer 114
B) Non-maleficence

Explanation 114
In situations where a minor client discloses experiencing bullying, the therapist's primary ethical concern is to prevent harm to the client and ensure their safety, aligning with the principle of non-maleficence.

Question 115
A therapist is considering offering group therapy services. What ethical principle should guide the therapist's approach to ensuring the well-being and safety of group members?
A) Beneficence
B) Autonomy
C) Non-maleficence
D) Professional boundaries

Answer 115
A) Beneficence

Explanation 115

Ensuring the well-being and safety of group members in group therapy is guided by the ethical principle of beneficence, aiming to promote their emotional health and support.

Question 116
A therapist is working with a client who is struggling with substance abuse and has a history of legal issues. What ethical principle should guide the therapist's approach to addressing both the addiction and legal concerns?
A) Autonomy
B) Non-maleficence
C) Beneficence
D) Professional boundaries

Answer 116
B) Non-maleficence

Explanation 116
When working with a client struggling with substance abuse and legal issues, the therapist's primary concern is to prevent harm and avoid exacerbating the client's issues, which aligns with the principle of non-maleficence.

Question 117
A therapist is working with a client who is experiencing significant distress related to their immigration status. What ethical principle should guide the therapist's approach to providing support and counseling?
A) Beneficence
B) Autonomy
C) Non-maleficence
D) Professional boundaries

Answer 117
A) Beneficence

Explanation 117
Supporting a client who is experiencing distress related to their immigration status is guided by the principle of beneficence, aiming to promote the client's well-being and emotional stability.

Question 118
A therapist is considering using narrative therapy techniques with a client. What ethical principle should guide the therapist's choice of therapeutic approach?
A) Autonomy
B) Non-maleficence
C) Beneficence
D) Professional boundaries

Answer 118
A) Autonomy

Explanation 118
The therapist's choice to use narrative therapy techniques should align with the principle of autonomy, allowing the client to shape their own therapeutic narrative.

Question 119
A therapist is working with a client who is struggling with issues related to their cultural identity. What ethical principle should guide the therapist's approach to providing culturally competent therapy?
A) Beneficence
B) Autonomy
C) Non-maleficence
D) Professional boundaries

Answer 119
B) Autonomy

Explanation 119
Providing culturally competent therapy that respects the client's cultural identity is guided by the principle of autonomy, allowing the client to maintain their cultural preferences and values.

Question 120

A therapist is working with a client who is experiencing grief and loss. What ethical principle should guide the therapist's approach to supporting the client through the grieving process?

A) Beneficence
B) Autonomy
C) Non-maleficence
D) Professional boundaries

Answer 120
A) Beneficence

Explanation 120
Supporting a client experiencing grief and loss is guided by the principle of beneficence, focusing on promoting the client's emotional well-being and coping.

Question 121

A therapist is considering providing online therapy services. What ethical principle should guide the therapist's actions to ensure the confidentiality and security of online therapy sessions?

A) Autonomy
B) Non-maleficence
C) Confidentiality
D) Professional boundaries

Answer 121
C) Confidentiality

Explanation 121
Ensuring the confidentiality and security of online therapy sessions is guided by the ethical principle of confidentiality.

Question 122

A therapist is working with a client who has been involved in a recent traumatic incident. What ethical principle should guide the therapist's approach to addressing the trauma and providing support?

A) Beneficence
B) Autonomy
C) Non-maleficence

D) Veracity

Answer 122
A) Beneficence

Explanation 122
Supporting a client who has been involved in a traumatic incident is guided by the principle of beneficence, aiming to promote the client's well-being and healing.

Question 123
A therapist is working with a couple, and one partner has a history of emotional abuse. What ethical principle should guide the therapist's approach to addressing emotional abuse within the relationship?
A) Autonomy
B) Non-maleficence
C) Beneficence
D) Professional boundaries

Answer 123
C) Beneficence

Explanation 123
The therapist's ethical duty in addressing emotional abuse within the relationship is to promote the well-being and safety of the couple, aligning with the principle of beneficence.

Question 124
A therapist is considering using play therapy techniques with a child client. What ethical principle should guide the therapist's choice of therapeutic approach?
A) Non-maleficence
B) Autonomy
C) Beneficence
D) Professional boundaries

Answer 124
C) Beneficence

Explanation 124

The therapist's choice to use play therapy techniques with a child client should align with the principle of beneficence, promoting the child's emotional well-being and development.

Question 125
A therapist is working with a client who is hesitant to disclose their history of self-harm due to feelings of shame. What ethical principle should guide the therapist's approach to creating a safe and non-judgmental environment for the client?
A) Autonomy
B) Non-maleficence
C) Beneficence
D) Professional boundaries

Answer 125
C) Beneficence

Explanation 125
Creating a safe and non-judgmental environment for a client who is hesitant to disclose their history of self-harm aligns with the principle of beneficence, promoting their emotional well-being and comfort.

Question 126
A therapist is working with a client who is struggling with issues related to their body image. What ethical principle should guide the therapist's approach to addressing body image concerns?
A) Beneficence
B) Autonomy
C) Non-maleficence
D) Professional boundaries

Answer 126
A) Beneficence

Explanation 126
Addressing a client's body image concerns is guided by the principle of beneficence, aiming to promote the client's well-being and self-acceptance.

Question 127

A therapist is considering offering art therapy techniques to a client with a history of trauma. What ethical principle should guide the therapist's choice of therapeutic approach?

A) Autonomy
B) Non-maleficence
C) Beneficence
D) Professional boundaries

Answer 127
A) Autonomy

Explanation 127
The therapist's choice to offer art therapy techniques should align with the principle of autonomy, allowing the client to choose therapeutic modalities that are comfortable for them.

Question 128

A therapist is working with a couple who is experiencing communication difficulties. What ethical principle should guide the therapist's approach to improving communication within the relationship?

A) Beneficence
B) Autonomy
C) Non-maleficence
D) Professional boundaries

Answer 128
A) Beneficence

Explanation 128
The therapist's ethical duty in improving communication within the relationship is to promote the well-being and harmony of the couple, aligning with the principle of beneficence.

Question 129

A therapist is considering providing therapy to a family dealing with a child's behavioral issues. What ethical principle should guide the therapist's approach to maintaining the best interests of the child and the family?

A) Autonomy
B) Non-maleficence

C) Beneficence
D) Professional boundaries

Answer 129
C) Beneficence

Explanation 129
Maintaining the best interests of the child and the family during therapy is guided by the ethical principle of beneficence, aiming to promote their emotional well-being and positive outcomes.

Question 130
A therapist is working with a client who has been involved in a recent traumatic incident. What ethical principle should guide the therapist's approach to addressing trauma and providing evidence-based interventions?
A) Beneficence
B) Autonomy
C) Non-maleficence
D) Veracity

Answer 130
A) Beneficence

Explanation 130
Supporting a client who has been involved in a traumatic incident and providing evidence-based interventions is guided by the principle of beneficence, aiming to promote the client's well-being and healing.

Question 131
A therapist is working with a couple who is experiencing infertility issues and is considering adoption. What ethical principle should guide the therapist's approach to supporting the couple's decision?
A) Autonomy
B) Beneficence
C) Non-maleficence
D) Professional boundaries

Answer 131
A) Autonomy

Explanation 131
Supporting the couple's decision regarding adoption should be guided by the principle of autonomy, respecting their ability to make choices about their family planning.

Question 132
A therapist is working with a client who is a minor and has disclosed experiencing bullying at school. What ethical principle should guide the therapist's actions in this situation?
A) Autonomy
B) Non-maleficence
C) Beneficence
D) Veracity

Answer 132
B) Non-maleficence

Explanation 132
In situations where a minor client discloses experiencing bullying, the therapist's primary ethical concern is to prevent harm to the client and ensure their safety, aligning with the principle of non-maleficence.

Question 133
A therapist is considering offering group therapy services. What ethical principle should guide the therapist's approach to ensuring the well-being and safety of group members?
A) Beneficence
B) Autonomy
C) Non-maleficence
D) Professional boundaries

Answer 133
A) Beneficence

Explanation 133
Ensuring the well-being and safety of group members in group therapy is guided by the ethical principle of beneficence, aiming to promote their emotional health and support.

Question 134

A therapist is working with a client who is struggling with substance abuse and has a history of legal issues. What ethical principle should guide the therapist's approach to addressing both the addiction and legal concerns?
A) Autonomy
B) Non-maleficence
C) Beneficence
D) Professional boundaries

Answer 134
B) Non-maleficence

Explanation 134
When working with a client struggling with substance abuse and legal issues, the therapist's primary concern is to prevent harm and avoid exacerbating the client's issues, which aligns with the principle of non-maleficence.

Question 135

A therapist is working with a client who is experiencing significant distress related to their immigration status. What ethical principle should guide the therapist's approach to providing support and counseling?
A) Beneficence
B) Autonomy
C) Non-maleficence
D) Professional boundaries

Answer 135
A) Beneficence

Explanation 135
Supporting a client who is experiencing distress related to their immigration status is guided by the principle of beneficence, aiming to promote the client's well-being and emotional stability.

Question 136

A therapist is considering using narrative therapy techniques with a client. What ethical principle should guide the therapist's choice of therapeutic approach?

A) Autonomy
B) Non-maleficence
C) Beneficence
D) Professional boundaries

Answer 136
A) Autonomy

Explanation 136
The therapist's choice to use narrative therapy techniques should align with the principle of autonomy, allowing the client to shape their own therapeutic narrative.

Question 137

A therapist is working with a client who is struggling with issues related to their cultural identity. What ethical principle should guide the therapist's approach to providing culturally competent therapy?

A) Beneficence
B) Autonomy
C) Non-maleficence
D) Professional boundaries

Answer 137
B) Autonomy

Explanation 137
Providing culturally competent therapy that respects the client's cultural identity is guided by the principle of autonomy, allowing the client to maintain their cultural preferences and values.

Question 138

A therapist is working with a client who is experiencing grief and loss. What ethical principle should guide the therapist's approach to supporting the client through the grieving process?

A) Beneficence
B) Autonomy

C) Non-maleficence
D) Professional boundaries

Answer 138
A) Beneficence

Explanation 138
Supporting a client experiencing grief and loss is guided by the principle of beneficence, focusing on promoting the client's emotional well-being and coping.

Question 139
A therapist is considering providing online therapy services. What ethical principle should guide the therapist's actions to ensure the confidentiality and security of online therapy sessions?
A) Autonomy
B) Non-maleficence
C) Confidentiality
D) Professional boundaries

Answer 139
C) Confidentiality

Explanation 139
Ensuring the confidentiality and security of online therapy sessions is guided by the ethical principle of confidentiality.

Question 140
A therapist is working with a couple, and one partner has a history of emotional abuse. What ethical principle should guide the therapist's approach to addressing emotional abuse within the relationship?
A) Autonomy
B) Non-maleficence
C) Beneficence
D) Professional boundaries

Answer 140
C) Beneficence

Explanation 140

The therapist's ethical duty in addressing emotional abuse within the relationship is to promote the well-being and safety of the couple, aligning with the principle of beneficence.

Question 141
A therapist is working with a couple who is considering divorce. What ethical principle should guide the therapist's approach to helping the couple navigate their decision?
A) Autonomy
B) Beneficence
C) Non-maleficence
D) Professional boundaries

Answer 141
A) Autonomy

Explanation 141
When a couple is considering divorce, the therapist should respect the autonomy of each partner in making decisions about their relationship.

Question 142
A therapist is working with a client who has a history of self-harm and suicidal thoughts. What ethical principle should guide the therapist's approach to ensuring the client's safety?
A) Beneficence
B) Autonomy
C) Non-maleficence
D) Veracity

Answer 142
C) Non-maleficence

Explanation 142
In situations involving self-harm and suicidal thoughts, the therapist's primary ethical concern is to prevent harm and ensure the client's safety, aligning with the principle of non-maleficence.

Question 143

A therapist is considering using play therapy techniques with a child client. What ethical principle should guide the therapist's choice of therapeutic approach?
A) Beneficence
B) Autonomy
C) Non-maleficence
D) Professional boundaries

Answer 143
B) Autonomy

Explanation 143
The therapist's choice to use play therapy techniques should align with the principle of autonomy, allowing the child client to engage in a therapeutic approach suitable for them.

Question 144

A therapist is working with a client who has been involved in a recent car accident. What ethical principle should guide the therapist's approach to addressing trauma and post-traumatic stress?
A) Beneficence
B) Autonomy
C) Non-maleficence
D) Veracity

Answer 144
A) Beneficence

Explanation 144
Supporting a client who has experienced a traumatic incident, such as a car accident, is guided by the principle of beneficence, aiming to promote the client's well-being and healing.

Question 145

A therapist is working with a family with a child who has been diagnosed with a severe behavioral disorder. What ethical principle should guide the therapist's approach to treatment and support?
A) Autonomy
B) Beneficence

C) Non-maleficence
D) Professional boundaries

Answer 145
B) Beneficence

Explanation 145
The therapist's ethical duty when working with a family with a child who has a severe behavioral disorder is to promote the well-being and positive outcomes for the child and the family, aligning with the principle of beneficence.

Question 146
A therapist is considering using art therapy techniques with a client. What ethical principle should guide the therapist's choice of therapeutic approach?
A) Non-maleficence
B) Autonomy
C) Beneficence
D) Professional boundaries

Answer 146
C) Beneficence

Explanation 146
The therapist's choice to use art therapy techniques should align with the principle of beneficence, aiming to promote the client's well-being and emotional expression.

Question 147
A therapist is working with a client who is hesitant to discuss their past history of substance abuse due to concerns about judgment. What ethical principle should guide the therapist's approach to creating a non-judgmental and supportive environment?
A) Beneficence
B) Autonomy
C) Non-maleficence
D) Professional boundaries

Answer 147
A) Beneficence

Explanation 147
Creating a non-judgmental and supportive environment for a client who is
hesitant to discuss their history of substance abuse aligns with the principle of
beneficence, promoting their emotional well-being and comfort.

Question 148
A therapist is working with a client who is experiencing relationship issues and
has a history of infidelity. What ethical principle should guide the therapist's
approach to addressing trust and fidelity issues within the relationship?
A) Autonomy
B) Non-maleficence
C) Beneficence
D) Professional boundaries

Answer 148
C) Beneficence

Explanation 148
The therapist's ethical duty in addressing trust and fidelity issues in the
relationship is to promote the well-being and healing of the couple, aligning
with the principle of beneficence.

Question 149
A therapist is considering using mindfulness-based therapy techniques with a
client. What ethical principle should guide the therapist's choice of therapeutic
approach?
A) Autonomy
B) Non-maleficence
C) Beneficence
D) Professional boundaries

Answer 149
C) Beneficence

Explanation 149
The therapist's choice to use mindfulness-based therapy techniques should
align with the principle of beneficence, promoting the client's emotional
well-being and self-awareness.

Question 150

A therapist is working with a client who is hesitant to disclose a recent crime they committed. What ethical principle should guide the therapist's approach to addressing this issue?

A) Autonomy
B) Non-maleficence
C) Beneficence
D) Professional boundaries

Answer 150
A) Autonomy

Explanation 150
Respecting the client's autonomy and choice to disclose a recent crime is an ethical consideration in this situation.

Question 151

A therapist is considering using family systems therapy techniques with a client. What ethical principle should guide the therapist's choice of therapeutic approach?

A) Non-maleficence
B) Beneficence
C) Autonomy
D) Professional boundaries

Answer 151
C) Autonomy

Explanation 151
The therapist's choice to use family systems therapy techniques should align with the principle of autonomy, allowing the client to shape their therapeutic process.

Question 152

A therapist is working with a client who is a minor and is considering an abortion. What ethical principle should guide the therapist's approach to supporting the client's decision?

A) Beneficence
B) Autonomy
C) Non-maleficence

D) Professional boundaries

Answer 152
B) Autonomy

Explanation 152
Supporting a minor client's decision regarding an abortion should be guided by the principle of autonomy, respecting their ability to make choices about their own body.

Question 153
A therapist is working with a client who is hesitant to share their gender identity due to fear of discrimination. What ethical principle should guide the therapist's approach to creating a safe and supportive environment for the client?
A) Beneficence
B) Autonomy
C) Non-maleficence
D) Professional boundaries

Answer 153
A) Beneficence

Explanation 153
Creating a safe and supportive environment for a client who is hesitant to share their gender identity aligns with the principle of beneficence, promoting their emotional well-being and comfort.

Question 154
A therapist is working with a client who has a history of substance abuse. What ethical principle should guide the therapist's approach to addressing the client's addiction issues?
A) Autonomy
B) Beneficence
C) Non-maleficence
D) Professional boundaries

Answer 154
C) Non-maleficence

Explanation 154
Addressing a client's addiction issues involves preventing harm and ensuring the client's safety, which aligns with the principle of non-maleficence.

Question 155
A therapist is considering offering online therapy services. What ethical principle should guide the therapist's actions to maintain the confidentiality and security of online sessions?
A) Autonomy
B) Non-maleficence
C) Confidentiality
D) Professional boundaries

Answer 155
C) Confidentiality

Explanation 155
Maintaining the confidentiality and security of online therapy sessions is guided by the ethical principle of confidentiality.

Question 156
A therapist is working with a client who is experiencing severe anxiety. What ethical principle should guide the therapist's approach to providing evidence-based treatment for anxiety disorders?
A) Beneficence
B) Autonomy
C) Non-maleficence
D) Veracity

Answer 156
A) Beneficence

Explanation 156
Providing evidence-based treatment for severe anxiety aligns with the principle of beneficence, aiming to promote the client's well-being and mental health.

Question 157

A therapist is working with a couple who is experiencing financial stress. What ethical principle should guide the therapist's approach to addressing financial concerns within the relationship?

A) Autonomy
B) Non-maleficence
C) Beneficence
D) Professional boundaries

Answer 157
A) Autonomy

Explanation 157
Respecting the autonomy of the couple in addressing financial concerns within the relationship is an ethical consideration in this situation.

Question 158

A therapist is considering using solution-focused therapy techniques with a client. What ethical principle should guide the therapist's choice of therapeutic approach?

A) Beneficence
B) Autonomy
C) Non-maleficence
D) Professional boundaries

Answer 158
C) Non-maleficence

Explanation 158
The therapist's choice to use solution-focused therapy techniques should align with the principle of non-maleficence, aiming to prevent harm and provide effective solutions.

Question 159

A therapist is working with a family in therapy, and there are concerns about child abuse. What ethical principle should guide the therapist's actions in this situation?

A) Beneficence
B) Autonomy
C) Non-maleficence

D) Confidentiality

Answer 159
C) Non-maleficence

Explanation 159
In situations involving concerns about child abuse, the therapist's primary ethical concern is to prevent harm and ensure the safety of the child, aligning with the principle of non-maleficence.

Question 160
A therapist is working with a client who is struggling with issues related to their cultural identity. What ethical principle should guide the therapist's approach to providing culturally competent therapy?
A) Beneficence
B) Autonomy
C) Non-maleficence
D) Professional boundaries

Answer 160
B) Autonomy

Explanation 160
Providing culturally competent therapy that respects the client's cultural identity is guided by the principle of autonomy, allowing the client to maintain their cultural preferences and values.

Question 161
A therapist is considering offering group therapy services. What ethical principle should guide the therapist's approach to ensuring the well-being and safety of group members?
A) Beneficence
B) Autonomy
C) Non-maleficence
D) Professional boundaries

Answer 161
A) Beneficence

Explanation 161

Ensuring the well-being and safety of group members in group therapy is guided by the ethical principle of beneficence, aiming to promote their emotional health and support.

Question 162

A therapist is working with a client who is hesitant to disclose their history of self-harm due to feelings of shame. What ethical principle should guide the therapist's approach to creating a safe and non-judgmental environment for the client?

A) Autonomy
B) Non-maleficence
C) Beneficence
D) Professional boundaries

Answer 162
C) Beneficence

Explanation 162
Creating a safe and non-judgmental environment for a client who is hesitant to disclose their history of self-harm aligns with the principle of beneficence, promoting their emotional well-being and comfort.

Question 163

A therapist is working with a client who is struggling with issues related to their body image. What ethical principle should guide the therapist's approach to addressing body image concerns?

A) Beneficence
B) Autonomy
C) Non-maleficence
D) Professional boundaries

Answer 163
A) Beneficence

Explanation 163
Addressing a client's body image concerns is guided by the principle of beneficence, aiming to promote the client's well-being and self-acceptance.

Question 164

A therapist is considering using cognitive-behavioral therapy (CBT) techniques with a client. What ethical principle should guide the therapist's choice of therapeutic approach?

A) Autonomy
B) Non-maleficence
C) Beneficence
D) Professional boundaries

Answer 164
C) Beneficence

Explanation 164
The therapist's choice to use CBT techniques should align with the principle of beneficence, aiming to promote the client's well-being and mental health.

Question 165

A therapist is working with a client who is a minor and has disclosed experiencing bullying at school. What ethical principle should guide the therapist's actions in this situation?

A) Autonomy
B) Non-maleficence
C) Beneficence
D) Veracity

Answer 165
B) Non-maleficence

Explanation 165
In situations where a minor client discloses experiencing bullying, the therapist's primary ethical concern is to prevent harm to the client and ensure their safety, aligning with the principle of non-maleficence.

Question 166

A therapist is considering offering group therapy services. What ethical principle should guide the therapist's approach to ensuring the well-being and safety of group members?

A) Beneficence
B) Autonomy
C) Non-maleficence

D) Professional boundaries

Answer 166
A) Beneficence

Explanation 166
Ensuring the well-being and safety of group members in group therapy is guided by the ethical principle of beneficence, aiming to promote their emotional health and support.

Question 167
A therapist is working with a client who is struggling with substance abuse and has a history of legal issues. What ethical principle should guide the therapist's approach to addressing both the addiction and legal concerns?
A) Autonomy
B) Non-maleficence
C) Beneficence
D) Professional boundaries

Answer 167
B) Non-maleficence

Explanation 167
When working with a client struggling with substance abuse and legal issues, the therapist's primary concern is to prevent harm and avoid exacerbating the client's issues, which aligns with the principle of non-maleficence.

Question 168
A therapist is working with a client who is experiencing significant distress related to their immigration status. What ethical principle should guide the therapist's approach to providing support and counseling?
A) Beneficence
B) Autonomy
C) Non-maleficence
D) Professional boundaries

Answer 168
A) Beneficence

Explanation 168

Supporting a client who is experiencing distress related to their immigration status is guided by the principle of beneficence, aiming to promote the client's well-being and emotional stability.

Question 169

A therapist is considering using narrative therapy techniques with a client. What ethical principle should guide the therapist's choice of therapeutic approach?
A) Autonomy
B) Non-maleficence
C) Beneficence
D) Professional boundaries

Answer 169
A) Autonomy

Explanation 169
The therapist's choice to use narrative therapy techniques should align with the principle of autonomy, allowing the client to shape their own therapeutic narrative.

Question 170

A therapist is working with a couple who is experiencing communication difficulties. What ethical principle should guide the therapist's approach to improving communication within the relationship?
A) Beneficence
B) Autonomy
C) Non-maleficence
D) Professional boundaries

Answer 170
A) Beneficence

Explanation 170
The therapist's ethical duty in improving communication within the relationship is to promote the well-being and harmony of the couple, aligning with the principle of beneficence.

Question 171
A therapist is considering providing therapy to a family dealing with a child's behavioral issues. What ethical principle should guide the therapist's approach to maintaining the best interests of the child and the family?
A) Autonomy
B) Non-maleficence
C) Beneficence
D) Professional boundaries

Answer 171
C) Beneficence

Explanation 171
Maintaining the best interests of the child and the family during therapy is guided by the ethical principle of beneficence, aiming to promote their emotional well-being and positive outcomes.

Question 172
A therapist is working with a client who has been involved in a recent traumatic incident. What ethical principle should guide the therapist's approach to addressing trauma and providing evidence-based interventions?
A) Beneficence
B) Autonomy
C) Non-maleficence
D) Veracity

Answer 172
A) Beneficence

Explanation 172
Supporting a client who has been involved in a traumatic incident and providing evidence-based interventions is guided by the principle of beneficence, aiming to promote the client's well-being and healing.

Question 173

A therapist is working with a couple who is experiencing infertility issues and is considering adoption. What ethical principle should guide the therapist's approach to supporting the couple's decision?

A) Autonomy
B) Beneficence
C) Non-maleficence
D) Professional boundaries

Answer 173
A) Autonomy

Explanation 173
Supporting the couple's decision regarding adoption should be guided by the principle of autonomy, respecting their ability to make choices about their family planning.

Question 174

A therapist is working with a client who is a minor and has disclosed experiencing bullying at school. What ethical principle should guide the therapist's actions in this situation?

A) Autonomy
B) Non-maleficence
C) Beneficence
D) Veracity

Answer 174
B) Non-maleficence

Explanation 174
In situations where a minor client discloses experiencing bullying, the therapist's primary ethical concern is to prevent harm to the client and ensure their safety, aligning with the principle of non-maleficence.

Question 175

A therapist is considering offering group therapy services. What ethical principle should guide the therapist's approach to ensuring the well-being and safety of group members?

A) Beneficence
B) Autonomy

C) Non-maleficence
D) Professional boundaries

Answer 175
A) Beneficence

Explanation 175
Ensuring the well-being and safety of group members in group therapy is guided by the ethical principle of beneficence, aiming to promote their emotional health and support.

Question 176
A therapist is working with a client who is struggling with substance abuse and has a history of legal issues. What ethical principle should guide the therapist's approach to addressing both the addiction and legal concerns?
A) Autonomy
B) Non-maleficence
C) Beneficence
D) Professional boundaries

Answer 176
B) Non-maleficence

Explanation 176
When working with a client struggling with substance abuse and legal issues, the therapist's primary concern is to prevent harm and avoid exacerbating the client's issues, which aligns with the principle of non-maleficence.

Question 177
A therapist is working with a client who is experiencing significant distress related to their immigration status. What ethical principle should guide the therapist's approach to providing support and counseling?
A) Beneficence
B) Autonomy
C) Non-maleficence
D) Professional boundaries

Answer 177
A) Beneficence

Explanation 177
Supporting a client who is experiencing distress related to their immigration status is guided by the principle of beneficence, aiming to promote the client's well-being and emotional stability.

Question 178
A therapist is considering using narrative therapy techniques with a client. What ethical principle should guide the therapist's choice of therapeutic approach?
A) Autonomy
B) Non-maleficence
C) Beneficence
D) Professional boundaries

Answer 178
A) Autonomy

Explanation 178
The therapist's choice to use narrative therapy techniques should align with the principle of autonomy, allowing the client to shape their own therapeutic narrative.

Question 179
A therapist is working with a couple who is experiencing communication difficulties. What ethical principle should guide the therapist's approach to improving communication within the relationship?
A) Beneficence
B) Autonomy
C) Non-maleficence
D) Professional boundaries

Answer 179
A) Beneficence

Explanation 179
The therapist's ethical duty in improving communication within the relationship is to promote the well-being and harmony of the couple, aligning with the principle of beneficence.

Question 180

A therapist is considering providing therapy to a family dealing with a child's behavioral issues. What ethical principle should guide the therapist's approach to maintaining the best interests of the child and the family?
A) Autonomy
B) Non-maleficence
C) Beneficence
D) Professional boundaries

Answer 180
C) Beneficence

Explanation 180
Maintaining the best interests of the child and the family during therapy is guided by the ethical principle of beneficence, aiming to promote their emotional well-being and positive outcomes.

Question 181

A therapist is working with a client who has been involved in a recent traumatic incident. What ethical principle should guide the therapist's approach to addressing trauma and providing evidence-based interventions?
A) Beneficence
B) Autonomy
C) Non-maleficence
D) Veracity

Answer 181
A) Beneficence

Explanation 181
Supporting a client who has been involved in a traumatic incident and providing evidence-based interventions is guided by the principle of beneficence, aiming to promote the client's well-being and healing.

Question 182

A therapist is working with a couple who is experiencing infertility issues and is considering adoption. What ethical principle should guide the therapist's approach to supporting the couple's decision?

A) Autonomy

B) Beneficence

C) Non-maleficence

D) Professional boundaries

Answer 182

A) Autonomy

Explanation 182

Supporting the couple's decision regarding adoption should be guided by the principle of autonomy, respecting their ability to make choices about their family planning.

Question 183

A therapist is working with a client who is a minor and has disclosed experiencing bullying at school. What ethical principle should guide the therapist's actions in this situation?

A) Autonomy

B) Non-maleficence

C) Beneficence

D) Veracity

Answer 183

B) Non-maleficence

Explanation 183

In situations where a minor client discloses experiencing bullying, the therapist's primary ethical concern is to prevent harm to the client and ensure their safety, aligning with the principle of non-maleficence.

Question 184
A therapist is considering offering group therapy services. What ethical principle should guide the therapist's approach to ensuring the well-being and safety of group members?
A) Beneficence
B) Autonomy
C) Non-maleficence
D) Professional boundaries

Answer 184
A) Beneficence

Explanation 184
Ensuring the well-being and safety of group members in group therapy is guided by the ethical principle of beneficence, aiming to promote their emotional health and support.

Question 185
A therapist is working with a client who is struggling with substance abuse and has a history of legal issues. What ethical principle should guide the therapist's approach to addressing both the addiction and legal concerns?
A) Autonomy
B) Non-maleficence
C) Beneficence
D) Professional boundaries

Answer 185
B) Non-maleficence

Explanation 185
When working with a client struggling with substance abuse and legal issues, the therapist's primary concern is to prevent harm and avoid exacerbating the client's issues, which aligns with the principle of non-maleficence.

Question 186
A therapist is working with a client who is experiencing significant distress related to their immigration status. What ethical principle should guide the therapist's approach to providing support and counseling?
A) Beneficence
B) Autonomy
C) Non-maleficence
D) Professional boundaries

Answer 186
A) Beneficence

Explanation 186
Supporting a client who is experiencing distress related to their immigration status is guided by the principle of beneficence, aiming to promote the client's well-being and emotional stability.

Question 187
A therapist is considering using narrative therapy techniques with a client. What ethical principle should guide the therapist's choice of therapeutic approach?
A) Autonomy
B) Non-maleficence
C) Beneficence
D) Professional boundaries

Answer 187
A) Autonomy

Explanation 187
The therapist's choice to use narrative therapy techniques should align with the principle of autonomy, allowing the client to shape their own therapeutic narrative.

Question 188

A therapist is working with a couple who is experiencing communication difficulties. What ethical principle should guide the therapist's approach to improving communication within the relationship?

A) Beneficence
B) Autonomy
C) Non-maleficence
D) Professional boundaries

Answer 188
A) Beneficence

Explanation 188
The therapist's ethical duty in improving communication within the relationship is to promote the well-being and harmony of the couple, aligning with the principle of beneficence.

Question 189

A therapist is considering providing therapy to a family dealing with a child's behavioral issues. What ethical principle should guide the therapist's approach to maintaining the best interests of the child and the family?

A) Autonomy
B) Non-maleficence
C) Beneficence
D) Professional boundaries

Answer 189
C) Beneficence

Explanation 189
Maintaining the best interests of the child and the family during therapy is guided by the ethical principle of beneficence, aiming to promote their emotional well-being and positive outcomes.

Question 190

A therapist is working with a client who has been involved in a recent traumatic incident. What ethical principle should guide the therapist's approach to addressing trauma and providing evidence-based interventions?

A) Beneficence
B) Autonomy

C) Non-maleficence
D) Veracity

Answer 190
A) Beneficence

Explanation 190
Supporting a client who has been involved in a traumatic incident and providing evidence-based interventions is guided by the principle of beneficence, aiming to promote the client's well-being and healing.

Question 191
A therapist is working with a couple experiencing communication issues. The therapist observes that one partner frequently interrupts and dismisses the other's thoughts. What should the therapist address to promote healthier communication?
A) Non-verbal cues
B) Boundaries and respect
C) Mirroring techniques
D) Active listening

Answer 191
B) Boundaries and respect

Explanation 191
In a couple experiencing communication issues, addressing boundaries and respect is essential to promote healthier communication. Dismissing and interrupting a partner's thoughts can be disrespectful and hinder effective communication.

Question 192
A therapist is working with a family, and one member is resistant to participating in therapy. What therapeutic approach can the therapist use to engage the resistant family member?
A) Confrontation
B) Family sculpting
C) Reframing
D) Detriangulation

Answer 192

B) Family sculpting

Explanation 192
Family sculpting is a therapeutic approach that can be used to engage a resistant family member. It involves physically arranging family members to represent their perceptions, emotions, and roles within the family.

Question 193
A therapist is working with a client who is struggling with body image issues. The client often engages in negative self-talk related to their appearance. Which therapeutic technique can help the client challenge and change these negative thought patterns?
A) Role-playing
B) Cognitive restructuring
C) Mindfulness
D) Behavioral activation

Answer 193
B) Cognitive restructuring

Explanation 193
Cognitive restructuring is a therapeutic technique that can help the client challenge and change negative thought patterns related to body image. It involves identifying and changing irrational or negative beliefs.

Question 194
A therapist is working with a couple experiencing sexual intimacy issues. The therapist suggests sensate focus exercises to help them improve their physical connection. What is the primary goal of sensate focus exercises?
A) Promoting emotional intimacy
B) Enhancing communication
C) Building trust
D) Increasing sensory awareness

Answer 194
D) Increasing sensory awareness

Explanation 194

The primary goal of sensate focus exercises is to increase sensory awareness and help couples become more attuned to physical sensations and their partner's responses, which can improve sexual intimacy.

Question 195

A therapist is working with a family dealing with a child's oppositional behavior. What intervention strategy can the therapist use to promote positive behavior and reduce oppositional tendencies?
A) Token economy
B) Reflection
C) Free association
D) Cognitive dissonance

Answer 195
A) Token economy

Explanation 195
A token economy is an intervention strategy that uses tokens or points as rewards for positive behavior. It can be effective in promoting positive behavior and reducing oppositional tendencies in children.

Question 196

A therapist is working with a couple experiencing relationship conflicts. The therapist asks each partner to express their feelings and thoughts without interruption while the other listens actively. Which therapeutic technique is the therapist using?
A) Genogram
B) Communication skill-building
C) Active listening
D) Boundary setting

Answer 196
C) Active listening

Explanation 196
The therapist is using active listening as a therapeutic technique to improve communication within the couple. Active listening involves one partner expressing themselves while the other listens without interruption, demonstrating empathy and understanding.

Question 197

A therapist is working with a client who is struggling with generalized anxiety disorder (GAD). What therapeutic approach is commonly used to treat GAD by focusing on the identification and modification of cognitive distortions?
A) Systematic desensitization
B) Dialectical behavior therapy (DBT)
C) Rational emotive behavior therapy (REBT)
D) Structural family therapy

Answer 197
C) Rational emotive behavior therapy (REBT)

Explanation 197
Rational emotive behavior therapy (REBT) is commonly used to treat generalized anxiety disorder (GAD) by focusing on the identification and modification of cognitive distortions.

Question 198

A therapist is working with a couple who is experiencing sexual dysfunction in their relationship. The therapist introduces sensate focus exercises to improve their sexual intimacy. What is the primary purpose of sensate focus exercises in this context?
A) Enhancing emotional intimacy
B) Addressing attachment issues
C) Promoting physical arousal
D) Reducing performance anxiety

Answer 198
A) Enhancing emotional intimacy

Explanation 198
The primary purpose of sensate focus exercises in the context of sexual dysfunction is to enhance emotional intimacy between the couple, fostering trust and communication.

Question 199

A therapist is working with a family dealing with a child's oppositional behavior. The therapist uses time-out as an intervention to manage challenging behavior. What is the goal of using time-out in this context?
A) Promoting assertiveness

B) Encouraging communication

C) Reducing the frequency of oppositional behavior

D) Enhancing self-esteem

Answer 199

C) Reducing the frequency of oppositional behavior

Explanation 199

The goal of using time-out as an intervention for managing challenging behavior in a child is to reduce the frequency of oppositional behavior by providing consequences for such behavior.

Question 200

A therapist is working with a couple who is experiencing marital conflicts, including arguments about financial decisions. The therapist introduces a budgeting and financial planning exercise to improve financial communication. What is the primary purpose of this exercise?

A) Building trust

B) Enhancing emotional intimacy

C) Promoting financial responsibility

D) Reducing marital conflicts

Answer 200

C) Promoting financial responsibility

Explanation 200

The primary purpose of a budgeting and financial planning exercise in the context of marital conflicts related to finances is to promote financial responsibility and better financial decision-making.